The Assyrian Tragedy

The Assyrian Tragedy

Mar Eshai Shimun, XXIII Catholicos Patriarch

February 1934

Copyright © 2010 by Mar Shimun Memorial Foundation.

Library of Congress Control Number: 2010907796
ISBN: Hardcover   978-1-4535-1144-2
                Softcover   978-1-4535-1143-5
                Ebook   978-1-4535-1145-9

This book was printed in the United States of America.

78794

CONTENTS

Summary

Opinions and Facts

1. Assyrian Losses in the war I
2. Sir John Simon and the Assyrian massacre.. I
3. The Bishop of Ripon.. I
4. Sir Arnold Wilson's Testimony...II
5. Difference Between Armenian and Assyrian Massacre III

Chapter One—Historical summary of the Assyrian Church and people

6. Origin of Assyrians..1
7. Assyrians embrace Christianity. 1
8. Missionary Entreprise..1
9. Causes of Eclipse of the Church of the East..2
10. Liturgy and present position of the Church...2

Chapter Two—The Assyrians entry into the war 1914-18.

11. First Attack on the Assyrians 4
12. The Assyrians in the house of Lords *(a)* The Archbishop of
    Canterbury *(b)* Lord Noel-Buxton *(c)* The Earl of Listowel 5
13. Great Britain Recognises Assyrians as Ally 6
14. Colonel McCarthy's Mission to the Assyrians 6
15. French and Russian Testimonies 7
16. Assyrian Exodus Through Persia..8
17. British High Commissioner undertakes
    Safeguard Assyrian Interests...9

Chapter Three—The Mosul Wilayet and the Assyrians.

18. Turkey Claims the Mosul Wilayet 11
19. Jafar and Yasin Pashas Pledges 11
20. League of Nations Commission of Enquiry 1925...................12
21. Sir Henry Dobbs...12
22. Air Vice-Marshal Iraq..13
23. Colonel Commandant Dobbin 13
24. Sir Samuel Hoare 14

Chapter Four—The Assyrian Levies and Iraq's entry into the League of Nations.

25. Anglo-Iraq Treaty...16
26. Discussions of Permanent Mandates Commission Nov. 1930.........17
27. Britain shoulders moral responsibility. 19
28. Discussions of Permanent Mandates Commission Oct.-Nov. 1931. 19
29. Fallacious accusations against the Patriarch..........................21
30. The National petition...21
31. Sir Francis' letters to the Patriarch. 22
32. The Patriarch proceeds to Geneva Sept. 1932......................25
33. Contents of the National petition..26
34. Assyrians' critical position recognised. 27

Chapter Five—The Assyrian settlement in Iraq.

35. Assyrians unanimous to return to Hakkiari. 29
36. The suggested "Assyrian enclave".......................................29
37. Assyrians used against Kurds, Turks and Arabs. 30
38. Turkish invasion of Mosul stopped.....................................30
39. Repatriation of the Assyrians fails. 31
40. Tiyari and Tkhuma tribes occupy Hakkiari. 31
41. British officer's visits arouse Turkish animosity....................31
42. Sir Percy Cox' negotiations fail. 32
43. The "Z" plan..32
44. Assyrians levies garrison Kurdistan. 33
45. Arrival of Major D. B. Thomson in Iraq..............................33
46. Coercive measures become acute. 34
47. Distribution of Assyrian population. 34

Chapter Six—The Patriarch's "Temporal Power".

48. Why did Assyrian recognise their Patriarch as Temporal Leader. 36
49. When did the Patriarch practice Temporal Power. 36
50. Major Wilson recommends detention of Patriarch, Lady Surma and Yaku Malik Ismail. 37
51. Removal of the Patriarch to Baghdad. 37

Chapter Seven—The forced exodus to Syria.

52. Major Thomson a complete failure. 39
53. Speech of Mutasarrif, Mosul. 39
54. Iraq nationality papers 39
55. Col. Stafford notifies Assyrians to find a new home. 40
56. Lord Noel-Buxton and the French. 41
57. Major Thomson's speech. 41
58. First Assyrian group leave for Syria 41
59. The letter of July 23rd. 42
60. Iraqi Ministers remove their headquarters to Mosul preparatory to massacre. 42
61. The Holy war. 42
62. Assyrians attacked in the river Faish-khabur. 43
63. The Patriarch's protest of June 29th, 1933. 43
64. Iraqi aeroplane kills 3 officers. 43
65. Rev. Dr. John B. Panfil's testimony. 44

Chapter Eight—The massacre.

66. The stone case. 46
67. Removal of Assyrian police from Mosul. 46
68. Inauguration of the massacre. 47
69. The Simel massacre. 47
70. 65 villages, looted, destroyed or burnt. 48
71. Dismissal of Assyrians from British employment. 48
72. British aeroplanes take photographs of horrible scenes. 49
73. Report of Mr. Badeau, American missionary. 50
74. Report of Mr. R. C. Cumberland, American missionary. 53

Chapter Nine—The Patriarch's position vis-a-vis the massacre

75. The Patriarch cut off from Assyrians in Mosul................................56
76. Assyrian requests to set Patriarch free ignored............................56
77. Thomson discusses settlemend with levies. 56
78. British Ambassador undertakes stop massacre...............................57
79. Air Vice-Marshal prevented from establishing refugee camp...........57
80. Patriarch deported on August 18th...57
81. Assyrian chiefs banished. 58
82. Issue of laissez-passer conditional...58

Chapter Ten—The present Assyrian situation in Iraq.

83. The destitute in Dohuk after the massacre...................................59
84. The Mosul camp. 59
85. Victims of massacre in Mosul and villages. 60
86. Assyrian belongings before the massacre. 62
87. Material losses during and after the massacre................................62

The End.

88. Yasin's connection with the massacre. 63
89. Mar Shimun asks for independent commission of enquiry..............63
90. The Six Power Committee..63
91. Possible places of emigration 64
92. Kurdish-Assyrian enclave..64
93. Proposals to safeguard Assyrian interests during the interval...........65
94. An appeal to America..67
95. Resolution of the Six Power Committee. 67
96. The Assyrian levy problem. 69

EDITORIAL NOTE

The Assyrian Tragedy emerged by Mr. S. Michael of Chicago, Illinois in 1988. At the time of the original printing, it had not been confirmed that His Holiness Mar Eshai Shimun, XXIII, Catholicos Patriarch of the Church of the East was the author of this compilation addressing what was known as the Assyrian Question. Since then, it has been established that *The Assyrian Tragedy* was created in this summarized format by His Holiness Mar Eshai Shimun illustrating the correspondences on behalf of the Church of the East and the Assyrian nation during the period from 1927 to 1933, which captures the final years in Iraq. Aside from his efforts with the League of Nations and later, the United Nations, the historical significance of this work has emerged as one of the primary sources of empirical documentation available demonstrating His Holiness Mar Eshai Shimun's struggles to correct the tragic events from that period of time.

A Brief Biography of His Holiness, Mar Eshai Shimun, XXIII

His Holiness Mar Eshai Shimun XXIII, Catholicos Patriarch was the Supreme head of the Church of the East, its Universal Pastor and the 119th Patriarch based on the Apostolic succession. The official name of the Church is the Holy Apostolic and Catholic Church of the East. It was founded by the Apostles, St. Peter, St. Thomas, St. Thaddeus, St. Bartholomew and St. Mari of the Seventy.

His Holiness was born on February 26, 1908 in Qudchanis, the mountainous region located in southern Turkey. Mar Eshai Shimun was raised with great care having received the required theological and liturgical training by the late Archdeacon of the Patriarchate, the Very Reverend Thoma of Ashita and by the Patriarchs' uncle, the Bishop of Rustaqa, His Grace, Mar Yosip (Joseph) Khnanishoo. In 1920, upon the death of his uncle, Mar Poulus (Paul) Shimun, His Holiness was ordained Patriarch at the age of twelve. In recognition of his keen intelligence and capability, it was deemed critical to further his education and training so the Patriarch was sent to St. Augustine's College, Canterbury, England.

After completing that phase of his preparatory schooling, he was accepted at Westcott House, Cambridge University, where he specialized in History and Statecraft. His formal schooling under the auspices of academia ended abruptly in 1927 when his nation and Church required his presence and leadership. However, his informal education continued to evolve over the following two decades in which the harder school of adversity had illuminated and deepened his wisdom whilst maturing his personality. Experience is always a great teacher, and what a life of rich and varied experience His Holiness spent. Simply isolating two mere decades of his tenure, from 1927 to 1947 in which he worked tirelessly fighting for his Assyrian people would for some be their failing, however from those difficulties, His Holiness Mar Eshai Shimun emerged as a profound and substantive leader.

His Holiness arrived in the United States in 1940. In addition to his work that dealt with the Assyrian cause, he provided oversight and direction that resulted in the establishment of parishes, built churches, as well as edited and translated literature from Aramaic into English for the use of the Church in the United States and other countries. By doing so, he further promulgated the mission of the founding Apostles and sought to be an inclusive educator for this flock, so that the faithful could learn the ancient liturgy in a consistent way. During this same period, the Patriarch had consecrated several bishops, ordained many priests and deacons and created the first English speaking Assyrian parish in Seattle, Washington. His dedication and diligence resulted in a considerable presence for the Church of the East throughout the United States. However, his work did not simply end here. Perhaps the most important of His Holiness activities had been the Apostolic pastoral visits to the Churches in India, and the Middle Eastern countries.

Always on the move in Iraq, Cyprus, England, Switzerland and the United States, often in danger of his life he met with foreign diplomats and heads of states. Through his persistence, he created a world presence for the Assyrians by his representations to the League of Nations and later his appeals to the United Nations. All the while he was contacting world leaders and discussing with them the situation of the Assyrians, with his indefatigable energy and unfailing commitment to this cause. His Holiness' dogged persistence, in fact his life, centered only on his duty to save his hapless Assyrians and his beloved Church of the East from utter destruction and disintegration.

Prior to Mar Eshai Shimun's intervention, Assyrians living among their Islamic neighbor's shared a tenuous relationship that was firmly rooted in mistrust on both sides of this religious chasm. Therefore, in 1948 His Holiness made a revolutionary announcement of a new policy for the Assyrian people and the Church of the East. Through direct contact to embassy representatives of Middle Eastern countries in Washington and at the United Nations Headquarters, he broke down the walls of suspicion and misunderstanding. This new policy decreed Assyrians and members of the Church of the East all over the world to remain as loyal and faithful citizens of the countries in which they lived, something that had never been done before in our history. The result was electric. There were amiable responses from Syria, Lebanon, and Iran resulting in the establishment of cordial relations with these governments.

Most historic and significant were his trips to Iraq in 1970 and 1971 at the invitation of the Iraqi government. This unprecedented act sent waves of hope throughout the Assyrian community living in Iraq for it had been in 1933 that the Patriarch and his family were exiled and separated from the Assyrians by the British government. For thirty seven long years the Patriarch was forbidden ministering to his considerable flock in Iraq. These trips had resulted in the strengthening of the spirit of the clergy and those faithful Assyrians. Furthermore, the building of schools, churches and the establishment of a Seminary in Tehran, Iran, resulted only from his direction and guardianship.

His Holiness was a prolific scholar, an exemplary writer and a charismatic speaker. As early as 1926 at the age of 18, the Patriarch attended the Nicene Council Commemoration held at Westminster Abbey, London. The Church and State Conference held in Oxford and the Faith and Order Conference held in Edinburgh were both attended by His Holiness in 1937. The distinguished Athenaeum Club of London had bestowed upon His Holiness by conferring an honorary membership. He was also a member of the American Historical Society and other organizations as well as being a representative to the World Council of Churches and being a notable among those chronicled in the annals of *Who's Who* repeatedly. Numerous appeals and publications concerning the Assyrian Question, written by the Patriarch and presented to the various governments and international bodies, highlight him as a writer of distinction. Various Aramaic and Syriac books have been translated into English by the His Holiness, Mar Eshai Shimun, some of which are:

- ☐ Portions of the Aramaic Liturgy;
- ☐ The Book of Hymns and Praises;
- ☐ Synodical Rules of the Church of the East;
- ☐ The Book of Marganitha, a standard theological work of the Church of the East;
- ☐ The publication of the homilies of Mar Narsai, the great saint and scholar of the fifth century, in two volumes, numbering more than 1400 pages;
- ☐ along with seventy pages of introduction and critical apparatus in English by His Holiness as well as countless outstanding sermons on the historical doctrine of the Church of the East.

A subject matter expert in Ecclesiastical History and an authority on the History of Christianity in the Middle East and Far East, Mar Eshai Shimun was fluent and literate in both the Aramaic and modern Syriac languages. In 1940, Time Magazine wrote of his Holiness, "Cambridge educated, Mar Shimun also speaks perfect English." His scholarly discourses on Church History at international Ecclesiastical conferences at various Universities attracted worldwide attention.

The succession of the patriarchs from the d'Mar Shimun family was a custom that became institutionalized for over 658 years, of which Mar Eshai Shimun XXIII, Catholicos Patriarch was the last. For Mar Eshai Shimun, his term as Patriarch was mired with tremendous hardship and the tenure of his indefatigable work on behalf of the Church of the East and the Assyrian nation finally took its toll on him. Continuing the tradition of Apostolic succession in the family was impossible, for there were no d'Mar Shimun nephews to succeed him. His Holiness, ever mindful of his flock took the opportunity to take the growth and evolution of the glorious Church of the East to the next level by developing and proposing a plan for succession that was an electoral selection process not an inherited one. His proposal had been accepted. After 55 years of focused dedication, the Patriarch retired from active responsibilities. In 1973 His Holiness announced his resignation from the Patriarchal responsibilities and married. Today, aside from his sisters, brother and sister in law, nieces and nephews, he is survived by two children. It might not have been known broadly at the time, but the Patriarch had agreed to return to the Church to organize its affairs, at the request of the Bishops, including the Metropolitan Mar Yosip Khnanishu in 1975. Tragically, his return was not realized. A clandestine plot was concocted to assassinate His Holiness, Mar Eshai Shimun and carried out on November 6, 1975. An assassin gunned him down at the door of his home in San Jose, California. He was 67 years old.   Mar Eshai Shimun, XXIII, Catholicos Patriarch of the East was an innovative leader of the Church and the Assyrian people, well schooled in both the ecclesiastical aspects of his vocation as well as erudite and urbane in the complexities of geopolitical issues that affected the Middle East, the Church of the East and his Assyrian people. Always attuned to the needs of his flock and the nation, he mindfully navigated the ever changing geopolitical landscape with uncompromising ethics, integrity and superior leadership, the very hallmarks of his character. His ingrained spirituality and political sophistication set him apart as a true leader of distinction. Never has an Assyrian leader demonstrated such deftness and agility in managing both the secular and temporal affairs which portray his truly magnificent stewardship of the Assyrian people and the Church of the East.

Proceeds of the sale of this book go to the Mar Shimun Memorial Foundation, which was founded in early 1976, in the shocking aftermath of the assassination of Mar Eshai Shimun XXIII, Catholicos Patriarch. This foundation is devoted to the memory of Mar Eshai Shimun, whose mission included educating non-Assyrians on the plight of the Assyrian nation, and implementing Church reforms so that the Church of the East could flourish in the 20th century. By publishing various books, other print media and posthumous donations, the foundation is able to direct its proceeds to needy members of the Church of the East around the world and other philanthropic organizations. For more information on His Holiness Mar Eshai Shimun, XXIII, the Patriarchal family and the Mar Shimun Memorial foundation, please visit http://www.MarShimun.com

OPINIONS AND FACTS

Assyrian Losses in the war

1. No nationals of any of the belligerent countries escaped the horrors of the world conflict of 1914-18, but no nation lost exactly two thirds[1] of its numbers as did the Assyrian nation. And while admittedly the eleventh day of November, 1918 was celebrated to mark the end of human troubles and open a new page in the history of civilization, the Assyrian horizon was permitted to remain cloudy.

At the moment of writing, death is playing havoc with thousands of old men, women and children who have been rendered destitute as a result of a massacre which took place last August, and the blood of many innocent persons has not yet ceased to flow.

Sir John Simon and the Assyrian massacre

2. Sir John Simon, the British Foreign Minister, speaking at Geneva on October 14th, 1933, on the Assyrian massacre said:

> "... At the same time, those facts could not possibly be regarded as justifying the excesses which had been committed. The apportionment of blame, however, was a somewhat barren proceeding."

The Right Honourable Mr. L. S. Amery, then British Minister for the Colonies during the time of the murders committed in the Goyan area in 1924, pressed the League of Nations for an independent enquiry commission on the spot and, despite the refusal of the Turkish Government, General Laidoner of Esthonia was sent out for investigation.

The Bishop of Ripon

3. The Right Rev. E. A. Burroughs, D. D., Bishop of Ripon[2] has made the following statement:

" . . . But so lately as last August another blow fell on the good name and prestige of Great Britain, the full extent of which does not seem to be at all widely realised. I refer to the massacre of Assyrian Christians at Simel and elsewhere in Iraq. Two official bodies to which I belong happen to have had the whole tragic and (for us) humiliating story under detailed review last week; and through more personal channels, on which I can entirely rely though I must not even indicate them, I have had further assurance of the substantial truth of what I am going to say. The story is too long to relate: even the crucial incidents I can only give in barest outline. But I say, with a full sense of responsibility, that one could hardly conceive a situation more calculated to damage this country at the bar of world opinion as a betrayer of its friends. As such we have been held up to scorn in the Press of other nations.

"The circumstances which immediately led up to the Simel massacres are obscure and too complicated to unravel here. Be it noted, however, that last Friday (October 20th)[1] the Iraqi representative at Geneva at last admitted that the Iraqi regular troops had been guilty of 'excesses' in suppressing the alleged Assyrian 'revolt': thus eating publicly the earlier statements of his Government, denying all responsibility. The official story of the 'revolt' may therefore also be modified in due course. Be it noted also that, according to last Wednesday's (October 18th) Times, the Iraqi commandant responsible for the 'operations' against the Assyrians, Beqir Sidky, was on Tuesday last promoted to the rank of General and Pasha, and the value of this apology can be gauged. Then, in the light of these two facts together, judge of the adequacy of or otherwise Sir John Simon's cold statement which followed, blaming the Assyrians almost as much as the Iraqis, and seizing the apology as a good excuse for turning from 'the barren procedure of apportioning blame' to the problem of settling the Assyrians outside Iraq."

Sir Arnold Wilson's Testimony

4. Sir Arnold Wilson[2] dealing with the services rendered by the Assyrians states:

> "They gave their services freely, not to the Arab, but to the British Government, in the hope that a measure of justice would some day be vouchsafed to them. We had used them so freely against Turks, Arabs and Kurds alike."

Dr. Wigram[1] has stated:

> "Can it be said that we have played the game by those to whom we gave promises and who served us because they trusted those promises?"

Difference Between Armenian and Assyrian Massacre

5. The difference between the Armenian and the Assyrian massacres lies in the fact that in the case of the first every possible step was taken to denounce it, whilst in the second every imaginable precaution has and is being taken to confine, in vain, its sad news to the area still stained with Assyrian blood.

History is unbiassed and it devolves upon it to record this unparalleled tragedy which has resulted in the destruction of the majority of one of the oldest Christian people.

CHAPTER ONE

Historical summary of the Assyrian Church and people

Origin of Assyrians.

6. The present Assyrians are the direct descendents of the Assyrian Race which played an important role in world history.

After the fall of the Assyrian Empire in 606 B. C. the more important element of the Assyrians took refuge to the North of Nineveh the Assyrian capital in the fastnesses of Kurdistan, the place which was to remain their home for 2,500 years.

The physiognomy, traditions and customs still in existence among the Assyrians of the present day bear witness to this fact.

Assyrians embrace Christianity.

7. The life of the heathen Assyrians whose history is recorded in the Bible, was a series of battles. With the advent of Christianity, they were, however, among the first to embrace that Faith.

It was in the latter part of the first century A.D. that the Christian Faith was preached in Assyria by St. Thomas of the Twelve apostles and by Addai and Mari of the of the Seventy. At that date, the Church of the East (now erroneously called the Nestorian Church) was founded. Its Teachings, liturgy, consecration and traditions have been in practice, uninterruptedly, up to the present day.

Missionary Entreprise

8. The great missionary enterprise of this Church is recorded by many historians. Suffice to say, that innumerable relics which are to be found

throughout the East such as the famous monument of Singan-fu in China, bear witness to this fact.

By the 13th century, its Bishops extended from Damascus to Peking and from Tatari to Malabar in India; and the Church contributed towards the spreading of civilization and culture among all races which came within its sphere of activities. The famous universities of Urhai (now Urfa) and Edessa (now Nisibin) were attended by students from the remotest of countries.

Causes of Eclipse of the Church of the East

9. No other Christian Church in the world has undergone persecutions as did this Church, first from the Heathen and then from the Moslems. Persecution after persecution followed each other. Of these the massacre carried out by Tamerlane in 1400 A.D. resulted in the greatest calamity to this Church. But this was not the end. Further persecutions and proselytism still continued until the Church dwindled to its present pathetic condition. But, despite all that has taken place, it has preserved its Christian Faith and Teachings.

Liturgy and present position of the Church

10. The Services and liturgy of the Church were handed down from the time of the Apostles with very minor alterations. The liturgy of the Holy Communion is called "The liturgy of Addai" (Thadeus) and is in use to-day in the same form as was originally practiced.

All the religious services are written and conducted in Aramaic, the language spoken by Our Lord. Phrases which appear in their original form in every language in the New Testament such as:

Talitha Koum "Damsel arise"
Eil Eil Lmana Shbaktan "My God, My God, why hast Thou forsaken me

are in current use among, and familiar to the present Assyrians.

As a result of the war, the Church lost all that had excaped former persecutions. All irreplaceable manuscripts and other invaluable articles dating from the 3rd and 4th centuries disappeared. Over a thousand Churches and other institutions with their possessions were destroyed.

The final but none the less tragic blow came last August through the massacre conducted against the Assyrians by the Iraq Government, adopting the methods of Tamerlane. Thus history has repeated itself in this twentieth century.

———————

CHAPTER TWO

The Assyrians entry into the war 1914-18.

First Attack on the Assyrians

11. Simultaneously with the outbreak of war with Turkey, the neighbours of the Assyrians became restive, and on being instigated and encouraged by minor officials, the Assyrians in the districts of Albaq and Gawar[1] were attacked, looted and massacred.

Conciliatory measures proved of no avail, and the semi-independent Assyrian nation had no alternative, after due warning, but to retaliate. As a threat to the nation, the late Hormizd D'Mar Shimun, brother of the Patriarch at the time, then a student in Constantinople was executed in Mosul under the former Turkish rule. This was the definite sign of the Assyrian entry into the war and was not due to "religious propaganda which was apparently being disseminated by the Russians among the Nestorian Christians on the Turco-Persian border before the outbreak of war" as has recently been stated.

Anyone who has the slightest idea of the organization of the Assyrian Church would agree that such a mis-statement would not have been made as the Assyrian Church was aloof from that of Petrograd more than the Church of England from that of Rome, and Russian religious propaganda of such a nature and at such a time could only have had a reverse effect to the Russian policy in those regions. Nevertheless, the Russian Government was anxious to win the Assyrians over to the Allied side and therefore welcomed the Assyro/Turco-Kurdish fracas. This alliance was confirmed by British representatives on the spot as it will be narrated.

The Assyrians in the house of Lords (a) The Archbishop of Canterbury (b) Lord Noel-Buxton (c) The Earl of Listowel

12. His Grace the Archbishop of Canterbury has stated[1]:

"My Lords, I make no apology for putting down the Motion which stands in my name, for it deals with a matter which very directly affects the chivalry and honour of this country . . . It is sometimes said that it was not this country but Russia that invited the Assyrians to throw in their lot with the allied cause. That may be true, but what we have to remember is that it was because they had taken this risk, because they made themselves our comrades in the common cause, that they have suffered most of their recent calamities."

Lord Noel-Buxton.[2]

" . . . In our opinion, His Grace has raised a question which is of real public importance and which deserves very full publicity. I would only venture to add a word based on personal experience of the Assyrian question. Before the war, when I was travelling on the frontiers of Turkey and Persia, I had some acquaintance with the Assyrians, and what I learned there illustrates the appalling experiences through which that nation has passed, and which we ought to take into account when, as to-day, there is a tendency somewhat to obscure the question of our responsibility . . . The most Rev. Primate has fully shown to us the completeness of the responsibility which rests upon us. Sir Francis Humphrys astonished many of us by his reiterated statements, at the time of the handing over of the mandate, that he personally feared no risks of danger to the Assyrians, but he did not attempt to minimise the overwhelming responsibility which lay upon us for any evil events that might follow. Mr. Orts went so far as to say that the Mandates Commission would never have agreed to the change of status if the Commission had not had the absolute assurance of His Majesty's Government that the Assyrians were safe from possible danger. In this question it is not too much to say that the good name of our country is indeed at stake unless we show a determination to provide such security as is still possible for the Assyrians who remain."

The Earl of Listowel[1].

" . . . I should like to stress even more strongly than the most Rev. Primate and my noble friend who has preceded me the moral responsibility of the British Government for the welfare of the Assyrian people now scattered about Iraq. Both the preceding speakers have mentioned that the Assyrians fought on our side during the war, but I think neither of them have pointed out the enormous sacrifice that this small and great people made at that time . . . they lost altogether by the end of the War about two-thirds of their total number."

Great Britain Recognises Assyrians as Ally

13. Sir Percy Cox has made the following statement[1].

" . . . The Assyrians, who numbered about 35,000, were the more important element for they had been recognised as Allies by *Great Britain in the War*, and had been used by her in the campaign of 1919 in Kurdistan. A definite promise of settlement under a benevolent, if not a British government, had been made to them, and their land, if not within our administered area, was at least on the immediate frontier."

Colonel McCarthy's Mission to the Assyrians

14. Colonel J.J. McCarthy who headed the British Military Mission to Persia during the war and who came in contact with the Assyrians there states:

"I have sent a copy of a memorandum I have written on the Assyrian question from the time your people joined forces with us against the Turks in 1918 up till 6 months after the armistice was signed. I have made a strong point of the fact that your people were definitely promised by me, (acting under orders from headquarters of course) that they would have their country restored to them, and that my orders, and only reason for raising the Assyrian contingent in Hamadan in 1918 was to drive the Turk out and re-occupy the country.

"I *do* hope the Foreign office will do something and do it *now* and before it is too late. No good can come out of delaying matters and the British government should face the position and do the right thing. It is all very difficult I know but surely not impossible. After all England is a big Nation and we did I suppose win the war? However, we didn't lose it, and if we had there would have been a different story to tell.

"It is clearly our duty to fulfill promises made to people who stood by us when we were in urgent need of all the help forthcoming. We did not have too many staunch and loyal friends in the East in 1918! Few people realize what your unfortunate people suffered and are still suffering in return to their loyalty to England. I will do my best to make known the terrible hardships they suffered under my own eyes. Never shall I forget that retreat from Urumia when I met the panic-stricken people on the Bidjar road and never do I want to see anything like it again.

"One thing is now certain and that is they cannot be left to the tender mercies of the Arabs whose one ambition in life appears to be to destroy them. This of course was very obvious to anyone who cared to think long before the last trouble."

Captain Gracey is the British officer who promised the Assyrians their independence. Extracts from the following letters written by two senior foreign officials, a Frenchman and a Russian, who were closely associated with Capt. Gracey when he made the promise are more than adequate to demonstrate the truth.

French and Russian Testimonies

15.
Docteur Paul Caujole,
       3, rue Lemoine,   Boulogne,
Boulogne-sur-Seine.   Dated 19th, January, 1934.
       (Seine.)

In reply to your letter of 18th January, 1934.

I have precisely preserved, as a souvenir, the Conferences to which you allude without, of course, being able to state the date.

The Conference was held in Urumia in December 1917 or early in January 1918.

I was invited to the Conference in question and took part in it as did Mr. Nikitine, the Russian Vice-Consul in Urumia.

Captain Gracey who was acting under the orders of the Intelligence Service came specially for the purpose from Van, his headquarters, to encourage the Assyrians to organize their resistance of the Turks.

In the name of England, he undertook to furnish immediately funds necessary for the payment of the troops and Non-commissioned officers. For the future, he promised the proclamation of the Independence of the Assyrian people.

Sd. Paul Caujole,
Ex-Médecin-Chef de l'Ambulance
Française du Caucase.

Basile Nikitine,
Ancien Consul.
29, rue George-Sand, Paris (16ᵉ).
January 31st, 1934

I certify that Captain Gracey, committed for Armenia and Kurdistan, of the British Military Mission, attached to the General Staff of the Caucasian army, came from Van at the end of the year 1917 and held in Urumia a special meeting of the Assyrian and foreign representatives and invited the Assyrian people to take up arms. He solemnly promised them financial and political assistance of his Government, both during the War and after the final regulation of the peace.

Requested by Captain Gracey, I attended the meeting in my capacity as Russian Consul and together with the other Foreign Representatives, I declared that if the Assyrians took up arms against the enemies, they could count after the war on making them obtain their independence which they would have well merited.

Sd. Basile Nikitine.

Assyrian Exodus Through Persia

16. After Capt. Gracey making his declaration, flying officer Pennigton (British) visited the Assyrians in 1918 for the same object, promising them finance and war material which never reached them. The Assyrians were told that they could join the British in Sain Qala. An Assyrian force of some 1,000 strong forced their way through, arriving at the promised place which was evacuated by the British some few days earlier. The Assyrians after another attempt were able to locate the British when they

all returned to Sain Qala and it was here that the rest of the Nation joined the English, since owing to lack of ammunition they were no longer able to hold their own against overwhelming odds. They did not reach Sain Qala, however, without more fighting on the way. Some ninety thousand persons, including some Armenians, left Urumia closely followed by the enemy troops through hostile territory, travelling day and night, with practically no food and no water for several days. Some thousands perished in this exodus through starvation, disease and massacre. Others were taken in captivity. As a result of this terrible journey which lasted 25 days, 7,000 more Assyrians died after their arrival in the British camp at ba'qubah, despite the care taken of them. Nevertheless, everybody, English and Assyrian, withdrew from Sain Qala to Hamadan in southern Persia when a strong Assyrian contingent was raised as narrated by Col. McCarthy and was used in Kurdistan, north of Iraq, to uphold the British authority over that turbulent area.

The families of the people were taken to Ba'qubah in Mesopotamia (now Iraq), and no doubt they were well cared for for about year—for which the Assyrians have never failed to express their gratitude.

On the other hand, the British Government recognised the services rendered by the Assyrians as it will be seen from the following letter written by the British High Commissioner, Iraq, for the information of the Assyrians.

D.O.No.S.O./1128.   The Residency,
                                          Baghdad, 1st May, 1924.

British High Commissioner undertakes Safeguard Assyrian Interests

17. . . . . "His Britannic Majesty's Government have given the most careful consideration for sometime to the question of safeguarding the interests of the Assyrian people, keeping in view both the services which they rendered to the Allied Cause during the war and their future relations with the Iraq government."

At the time this letter was written the Turks were pressing hard their claim to Mosul and its unexploited mines so essential to Great Britain, and it was necessary to enlist the help and co-operation of the Assyrians. Hence these letters, none of which, unfortunately, have been kept. And when the

Mosul dispute was over, the tide turned against the Assyrians and they were finally deserted to suffer martyrdom at the hands of the Iraq government whose internal disorders they were called upon time after time by the British mandatory Power to quell.

CHAPTER THREE

The Mosul Wilayet and the Assyrians.

Turkey Claims the Mosul Wilayet

18. As already stated, the Turks claimed the whole of the Mosul Wilayet which was occupied by the British forces after the armistice, and its fate depended on the choice of the inhabitants of the disputed territory. Although the Assyrians were small in number, nevertheless, having been stampeded out of their original home in Turkey, there was wide sympathy for them. This is, however, not the place to go into the details of this question.

The Turks massed troops on the frontier of the disputed territory with a view to its occupation and thus to make the whole issue a fait accompli and to force their claim on their opponents. The Iraq army was totally unfit to defend the artificial borders of Iraq and the burden of guarding those dangerous frontiers fell on the shoulders of the Assyrians. Both politically and from the military point of view, the Assyrians were largely responsible for the annexation of the Wilayet to Iraq rather than to Turkey.

But the Assyrians did not throw in their lot with Iraq and the mandatory Power without having first obtained assurances that their future would be adequately safeguarded. Had it not been for those assurances, the Assyrians and all the remaining inhabitants would have preferred Turkish to Arab rule.

Jafar and Yasin Pashas Pledges

19. One of those assurances as quoted by Sir Henry Dobbs[1] who was His Britannic Majesty's Government representative in Iraq at the time of the frontier dispute was this:

"In order to reassure them (The Assyrians) as to their future, two successive Iraq cabinets, those of Jafar Pasha and of Yasin Pasha, officially pledged the Government of Iraq to provide lands in Iraq for those Assyrians who might be dispossessed of their original homes by the decision of the

League of Nations and to devise a system of administration for them which would ensure to them the utmost possible freedom from interference.

"It can hardly be doubted that this liberal attitude on the part of the Iraq government had its influence on the deliberations of the Frontier Commission."

This assurance was given before the arrival of the League of Nations Frontier Commission, which later embodied the following recommendation in its report:[1]

League of Nations Commission of Enquiry 1925

20. "Since the disputed territory will in any case be under the sovereignty of a Moslem State, it is essential in order to satisfy the aspirations of the minorities—notable the Christians, but also the Jews and Yazidi—that measure should be taken for their protection.

"It is not within our competence to enumerate all the conditions which would have to be imposed on the Sovereign State for the protection of these minorities. We feel it our duty, however, to point out that the Assyrians should be guaranteed the re-establishment of the ancient privileges which they possessed in practice, if not officially, before the war. Whichever may be the Sovereign State, it ought to grant these Assyrians a certain local autonomy, recognising their right to appoint their own officials and contenting itself with a tribute from them, paid through the agency of their Patriarch . . . The status of minorities would necessarily have to be adapted to the special conditions of the country; we think, however, that the arrangements made for the benefit of minorities might remain a dead letter if no effective supervision were exercised locally.

"The League of Nations representative on the spot might be entrusted with this supervision."

In addition to the resort quoted above, the following letters gave the Assyrians further hope that their interests would be safeguarded.

Sir Henry Dobbs

21. No. 9882.   The Residency,
                                                 Baghdad, 4th August 1923.

I have received your letter of 8th July, 1923 (O.S.) setting forth the anxiety of your people regarding their future. You can rest assured that this very important matter will have my closest attention and I hope that I may have an opportunity of discussing it with you personally before long. The British Government are fully aware of the services rendered by your people and of their difficulties and are very desirous of securing an arrangement which will safeguard their interests.

Sd. Henry Dobbs.

Air Vice-Marshal Iraq

22.
Air Headquarters,
British Forces in Iraq.
Baghdad, 28th January 1925.

Lieutenant-Colonel Barke has brought to my notice the great assistance and advice which you gave to him in the organisation of the Assyrian irregular troops on the Turco-Iraq frontier during the recent disturbances, and I wish to express to you, in the name of the British forces, my sincere thanks for your untiring efforts.

I should also be glad if you would convey to all members of the Assyrian Nation concerned my high appreciation of the manner in which they performed their duties, the high standard of which, will, I am sure, continue in the future.

Sd. Air Vice-Marshal.

Colonel Commandant Dobbin

23. No. 1121

Air Headquarters, Iraq levies.
Mosul
30th January 1925.

I have pleasure in sending you the following extract from the report of Lieutenant-Colonel C.R. Barke on the recent operations round Amadiyah.

"In accordance with verbal instructions from the Colonel-Commandant, I give below a list of names of those who rendered especially good service during the period covered by this report and my A.N./110 of 19-10-1924.

"I wish to mention the very great assistance rendered to me in the organisation of the irregulars by Lady Surma D'Beit Mar Shimun. That such large numbers returned to my assistance after their first withdrawal was largely due to her efforts and commands and throughout the whole period under report she gave invaluable help and advice in all matters concerning them."

Sd . . . Dobbin,
Colonel-Commandant.
Commanding, Iraq levies.

Sir Samuel Hoare

24.

Air Ministry
Gwydyr House
Whitehall S.W.I.
March 7th, 1926.

I write to wish you every success in your journey to America. You can rely upon Mr. Amery and myself to do everything in our power to ensure fair treatment for your people.

Sd. Samuel Hoare.

No. 13697.

The Residency,
Baghdad, the 30th November, 1928.

"I shall leave Iraq with the feeling that a dark chapter in the history of your people is closing and that guided by the wise counsels of your Beatitude they have before them a brighter and more prosperous future.

Sd. Henry Dobbs.

As prophecised by the League of Nations Frontier Commission, its recommendations for the welfare of the Assyrians remained a dead letter as no League Commissioner on the spot was appointed.

It cannot be said that the Assyrians did not warn those concerned that once the British influence was withdrawn, without effective guarantees for the future safety of the Assyrians, that their position would be made intolerable in Iraq. In writing the fears of the Assyrians were appreciated but nothing was done in practice to allay their apprehensions. The assyrians inundated the offices of the British officials and of the Secretariat of the League of Nations with alarming appeals not because they objected to the independence of Iraq but because they feared their future fate under Arab rule.

————————

CHAPTER FOUR

The Assyrian Levies and Iraq's entry into the League of Nations.

Anglo-Iraq Treaty.

25. On June 30, 1930, the Anglo-Iraq treaty was signed and it was *not* unnatural if the Assyrians were perturbed on discovering that the mandatory Power had made no provision for their safety and welfare in the future. On making representations to the British officials, they were told that the League of Nations would take sufficient guarantees for the protection of minorities.

As a result of agitations caused by Iraqi extremists against the Treaties which preceded that of 1930, the British High Commissioner was instructed in February 1929 to inform the Iraq Government that His Britannic Majesty's Government would be prepared to support the candidature of Iraq for admission to the League in 1932, "*without proviso or qualification*" hence the admission of Iraq in that year to the League as an independent State was already a *fait accompli*. The aim of the British Government was to ensure her own interests by means of the proposed treaty in an independent Iraq and no other consideration would deter her form achieving her twofold aim.

If the British Government had entrusted the League of Nations with the task of safeguarding the future of the Assyrians and had not tied the hands of the League, there is no doubt that the League would not have satisfied itself with "*scraps of papers*". But the British Government did not wish the minorities to obtain more than those *papers* and the League did not insist, for it was told that the *British moral responsibility* was behind those paper guarantees. Moreover, the British representative assured the League that Iraq was a *benevolent* and *tolerant* Government and that the paper guarantees were more than adequate, in a country like *Iraq*, to safeguard the Assyrian interests.

Iraq was admitted to the League on October 3rd, 1932, and *ten* months had not elapsed when the fears of the Permanent Mandates Commission which was being misled were, alas, substantiated.

While the British Government had determined to deliver the Assyrians unconditionally to the tender mercies of an unrestrained Iraq Government, it persisted in its disastrous policy of using the Assyrian levies for its own political and material ends.

The discussions of the Permanent Mandates Commission on the question under review are worth while recording. There is no sufficient space in the present pamphlet to accommodate all that the Permanent Mandates Commission has said, but the following quotations should give the reader a clear idea as to why the League of Nations was unable to press, for effective guarantees, more than it did for the future safety of the Assyrians.

Discussions of Permanent Mandates Commission

Nov. 1930.

26. The following is quoted from the League of Nations official No. C.643.M.262.1930.vi (Permanent Mandates Commission. Minutes of the nineteenth session held at Geneva from Nov. 4th to 19th, 1930).

M. Orts. In the case of Iraq, the mandatory Power stated that the country was ripe for independence, but in contrast to this favourable view there were those of the religious and racial minorities; it was clear that the latter regarded with a certain amount of *apprehension* the approaching termination of the mandate.

Major Hubert Young. My Govt. believes that the Iraqis are capable of accepting responsibility in full after the measures in process have been going on for two or three years, and have announced that *belief* both to the League and to the Iraq Govt.

Marquis Theodoli . . . and it might be inclined to think that Iraq was not quite so *ripe for independence* as the mandatory power appeared to imagine.

M. Rappard associated himself with the observations of M. Orts. It was the duty of the Commission to express an opinion on the question whether Iraq had proved its capacity to govern itself. His personal doubts on this subject had in no way been allayed by the information contained in the present report.

M. Orts asked whether the British officials will still have the same *influence* when this special position no longer exists.

Major Young. I believe that their influence will not only be maintained but will actually be *increased* . . . I personally believe that it will be even more readily accepted . . . and that the remaining reports will be of a nature to assure the commission that their apprehensions are *unfounded.*

Count de Penha Garcia. With regard to the governing class, he was under the impression that there were not *many* politicians in Iraq who would be capable of governing a country which would have to stand alone.

Major Young. The British Government appreciated the fact that they had undertaken *a very grave responsibility.* They would not have allowed any *pressure* to lead them to adopt a policy in Iraq which they believed would not succeed.

M. Orts pointed out that the British Government appeared to understand and the matter as follows: On July 31st, the Under-Secretary of State for the colonies, replying to a question asked in the House of Commons, had said: "We are satisfied that the Iraqi Government fully intend to give *liberal* treatment to their minority peoples and that full opportunity will be afforded them to preserve their own *language* and *culture.* We are also confident that the Iraqi Government will be in a position fully to satisfy the League of Nations on this point when the time comes.

Major Young . . . . For reasons it was unnecessary to enlarge, the British Government had sometimes felt, before its declaration of 1929, that it was difficult to press the Iraqi Government to move *faster* in the matter of the Assyrians *But the mandatory Power was convinced that the whole question would be definitely settled by* 1932 . . . It was the *firm* belief of the British Government that the Iraqi Government would be qualified for membership of the League by that date.

Count de Penha Garcia . . . The mandatory Power must give its consent, since it will, in reality, be *morally responsible* for the *consequences* of the termination of the mandate.

Following the above deliberations, the Permanent Mandates Commission reached the following conclusion:

"The Commission echoed the apprehensions felt, not only by the parties concerned, but also by a considerable section of the public in several countries regarding the lot of the minorities in Iraq since the moment the country began to prepare for complete independence, and the supervision of the Iraq Administration by the mandatory Power was gradually *relaxed.*"

During the discussion which took place between June 9th and June 27th, 1931, Sir Francis Humphrys, the High Commissioner in Iraq whose instructions were to admit Iraq to the League, in order to silence the members of the Permanent Mandates Commission made the following declaration on June 19th, 1931.

Britain shoulders moral responsibility.

27. *"His Majesty's Government fully realised its responsibility in recommending that Iraq should be admitted to the League of Nations which was in its view the only logical way of terminating the Mandate. Should Iraq prove herself unworthy of the confidence which had been placed in her the moral responsibility must rest on His Majesty's Government, which would not attempt to transfer it to the Mandates Commission."*

Discussions of Permanent Mandates Commission

Oct.-Nov. 1931.

28. During the discussions held at Geneva between October 26th, to November 13th, 1931, the members of the Permanent Mandates Commission despite Sir Francis, eminent declaration quoted above took up the question of the Minorities as it will be seen from the following remarks'

M. Palacios. As the Commission had no direct cognisance of Iraq and had only heard of its progress through statements made by Great Britain, and as, moreover, the Commission had received petitions and reports which raised objections and gave rise to anxiety with regard to the termination of the mandate, he wondered whether the attitude adopted by M. Van Rees at the last session was not the right one when he said that the mandatory Power should be left *full responsibility* for the statement that Iraq was now capable of managing her own affairs.

M. Van Rees observed that, during the June session, he had frequently had occasion to state that he was *not* in favour of a declaration being made by the Mandates Commission to the effect that Iraq was now in a position to govern itself.

Mlle *Dannevig.* Personally, she thought that the premature cessation of the mandate would be a *misfortune* for the country. She was afraid they might later on regret having, for *dominant reasons of policy*, emancipated the territory of Iraq before the proper time.

M. Rappard. None of the members of the Commission, even the most optimistic, would be *prepared* to affirm their conviction that Iraq could be emancipated without *disadvantage*.

M. Orts pointed out that the discussion had shown that, in any case, the members of the Commission appear to have very *little* confidence as to the way in which the Iraqi government would treat the *Minorities*.

Sir Francis Humphrys . . . The Arabs of Iraq are an essentially *tolerant* race, tolerant of other *races* and other *religions*. What grounds have we in the case of Iraq for assuming ill-will or bad faith? So far as I am aware, there have been no *instances* of religious persecution in Iraq. In little more than a decade, and from disperate material, a new nation has been fashioned, self-reliant, stable, imbued with a high spirit of patriotism and with enthusiasm to justify itself in the *eyes* of its peers; that, I submit, is an achievement of which the League of Nations and my Government have just cause for pride;
"You gentlemen, hold the *key* to the door through which this young State must pass to full manhood and emancipation. I ask you to *open* that door."

M. Orts asked if it were correct that the Assyrian Patriarch had supplied the High Commissioner with a list of *seventy-nine* unpunished cases of murder of Assyrians.

Sir Francis replied in the *affirmative*.

Mlle *Dannevig emphasised* the responsibility assumed by the mandatory Power, and reminded the Commission of the statement which the accredited representative had read on the psychological factor in Iraq. Like everyone else, she was anxious to create the best possible guarantees for the minorities. She feared, however, that, if additional guarantees were called for, the Mandatory Power might, *if trouble arose*, lay the responsibility on the Mandates Commission, which had gone beyond the recommendations of the mandatory Power and thereby prevented the latter from exercising the influence upon which it had relied."

In September 1931, the Patriarch sent in an application to the League of Nations setting forth the fears of the Assyrians for the future and definitely said that they shall be exterminated after the emancipation of Iraq, and that if no real remedy could be found before that date, the question of their *emigration* from Iraq to some other country or Syria under the French Government may be considered.

Such were the fears of the Assyrians and the unanimous views of the members of the Permanent Mandates Commission at the close of 1931. Now that Iraq was approaching independence, the situation of the Assyrians in Iraq was developing from bad to worse. The British representative, however, persisted in his assurances that neither the fears of the Permanent Mandates Commission nor the apprehensions of the Assyrians were founded.

Fallacious accusations against the Patriarch.

29. During April and May 1932, the Patriarch was lying dangerously ill in Baghdad and the British Government, on reports no doubt emanating from Sir Francis Humphrys, accused him quite recently[1] of having toured, for purposes of propaganda, among the Assyrian Levies.

The Assyrian chiefs were fully alive to the situation and decided to make a final attempt with a view to securing some *real* guarantees other than those of "paper" to be able to live in a compact community.

The Assyrian levies, still guarding the British aerodromes and the Iraq frontiers and whose families and immediate relatives would be involved soon after the emancipation of Iraq joined in the attempt and gave their British officers one month's notice in accordance with the service terms of their contracts. Sir Francis Humphrys was inclined to call this a *mutiny*. He found himself in a dilemma. The Anglo-Iraq treaty, which would come into operation on the emancipation of Iraq, forbids the employment as aerodrome guards of other than Iraqis. The replacement of Assyrian by British troops after emancipation would have been the first breach of the treaty.

The National petition

30. On June 17th, 1932, a petition from the Assyrian chiefs and the levies was forwarded to the League of Nations and the mandatory Power

demanding special safeguards for the near future before it was too late. On the question of the levies and the demands, extracts from the following letters written by Sir Francis Humphrys are interesting to quote. Moreover, Sir Francis encouraged the Patriarch to proceed to Geneva and pursue the Assyrian cause. Sir Francis did not only disregard his pledge that he would *do* all in his power to help the Assyrians but he in reality adopted an obstructive policy in every possible way.

Sir Francis' letters to the Patriarch.

31. No. S.O.841.   The Residency,
                                         Baghdad, 18th June 1932.

Your Beatitude,

. . . This petition[1] puts forward a number of demands of far reaching effect and great importance and raises issues which cannot be settled without a reference to the League of Nations.

In the meanwhile, your people have everything to lose from precipitate action and since, as I have shown, it is quite impracticable to make a reply to the petition by the 28th of June, I urge you to advise the Assyrian levies to postpone the execution of their resolution to cease serving, until such time as a reply is received from the League.

If your Beatitude does not so advise them, and if they persist in leaving the Levies and joining in the National movement, before an answer is given to you, I must warn Your Beatitude that the Assyrians will be regarded as having offered a grave discourtesy to the League, who will have been given no possible opportunity to reply before your ultimatum expires. Moreover, in such circumstances the Assyrians could not reasonably expect to obtain any future employment in the Government services.

Your sincere friend,
                                              F.H. Humphrys.

No. S.O.851.

The Residency,
                                         Baghdad, 22nd June, 1932.

Your Beatitude,

I have received your letter of the 20th of June by the hand of Captain Holt. I have informed your Beatitude that I am unable to understand what the Assyrians have to gain by giving up their present service, which is worth nearly a lakh of rupees a month to them, and by disqualifying themselves for further service in the future. On the other hand, they have a very great deal to lose by such short-sighted behaviour, which cannot fail to appear to the British Government and people as singularly ungrateful and inopportune. In giving such an ultimatum, Your Beatitude cannot fail to realise that the Assyrian leaders are putting themselves in the wrong with the British Government and the League of Nations.

There is nothing more for me to say in this matter, except to express my deep regret at the unnecessary sufferings which the Assyrians seem determined to bring on themselves.

I remain your sincere friend,
F.H. Humphrys.

High Commissioner's Office,
Baghdad, 28th June, 1932.

Your Beatitude,

It is impossible for me to give you a reply in precise terms as to what demands in the Assyrian petition will and what will not be considered as reasonable and in conformity with the general policy of my Government and the League. I cannot at this stage commit myself further than to inform you that such questions as recognition of Patriarch, land settlement, representation in Parliament, schools, dispensaries, retention of rifles, and conditions of service in the Iraq forces, are recognised by me as reasonable subjects for consideration and that the earliest and most sympathetic attention to these matters will be pressed by me on the Iraqi government and, through my government, on the League of Nations.

You may be assured of the sincere goodwill of the British government and myself and of our desire to do all that is possible for the welfare of the Assyrian people.

I remain your sincere friend,
F.H. Humphrys.

Personal.

The Residency,
Baghdad, June 28th, 1932.

Your Beatitude,

I was very glad to receive your message this evening. You know that I shall *do* everything in my power to help you and your people at Geneva. I will even do my best to find a solution in regard to Hakkiari though you will realise that this is an international question of great delicacy.

All I ask from Your Beatitude and the Assyrian leaders is that they should *assist me* by maintaining the levies in loyal service and the people in a calm spirit until the decision of the League of Nations has been received.

I know that I can rely on your help in this.

I am, your sincere friend,
F.H. Humphrys.

No. S.O.961.   High Commissioner's Office,
Baghdad, 15th July, 1932.

Your Beatitude,

I have forwarded to the Secretary of State the Assyrian petition of the 17th June, and the British Government are now in communication with the League Secretariat with a view to arranging for its early consideration by a competent League body.

Your sincere friend,
F.H. Humphrys.

Sar Amadiyah, 25th June, 1932.

His Excellency,
     Sir Francis Humphrys,
         High Commissioner for Iraq,
            Baghdad.

Excellency,

Reference your letter No. S.O.851 dated 22nd June 1932 which I received.

The leaders have already departed to their respective destinations.

I will promise to do my best in persuading the leaders to consent and the levies to prolong their services if your excellency will write and assure me on *your honour* that:

Your Excellency in the office you represent will do your utmost to support the demands stated in the national petition dated 17th June, 1932, in the following respective quarters, namely, Your Government, the Iraq Government and the League of Nations and also inform me of the future levy conditions.

The Assyrian Patriarch,
Mar Shimun.

Beatitude,

I have received your message of the 25th June. It is my duty to explain that some of the demands contained in the national petition of the 17th of June appear to be in conflict with the declared policy of my Government and the League. I undertake to support to the best of my ability with my government and the League of Nations those demands which appear to be reasonable and in conformity with the general policy of my government and the League.

Your sincere friend,
Francis Humphrys.

The Patriarch proceeds to Geneva Sept. 1932.

32. It was on this strict understanding that the British Government would *do* its best for the Assyrians at the League of Nations that the Patriarch proceeded, at the request of his people to Geneva, to see how far the promise would be kept.

The results of the discussion at Geneva of this question between November 3rd to December 6th, 1932, will be seen hereunder.

M. Orts. In fact, complaints continued to arrive from the racial and linguistic minorities in Iraq, regarding their situation in the country . . . It still remained that the Assyrian community showed the *greatest anxiety*, amounting almost to *despair*, at the prospect of the fate which awaited it when British control came to an End. The ambitions attributed to Mar Shimun were not a *sufficient* explanation of such a general and deep feeling.

Mr. Flood (British representative) . . . The Assyrians were now putting forward a series[1] of quite *impracticable* suggestions.

M. Orts. The signatories of the petitions of October 20th and 23rd, 1931, assert that it will be impossible for them to live in Iraq after the withdrawal of the mandate. They therefore ask that arrangements be made for the transfer of the Assyrians in Iraq to a country under the rule of the Western Nations, or, if this is not possible, to Syria.

The United Kingdom Government replied in its observations that, if the French Government, or any other European Government, were prepared to offer the Assyrians *compact accommodation*, to guarantee them *fair* and *permanent* conditions, and to finance their transport, and if the Assyrians themselves desired to accept the offer, neither the mandatory Power nor the Iraqi Government would object.

Such a contingency, however, seemed so *remote* that the United Kingdom Government did not think it *expedient* to take any steps in the matter."

Besides the claims of the Assyrian people referred to in Sir Francis' letter dated June 28, 1932, the petition of the Assyrians included the following which were much less than what the League of Nations said they had right to and much below the pledges made by the British Government. These were:

Contents of the National petition.

33. (*a*) That the Assyrians should be settled in a sub-division of the Mosul liwa in a compact community.

(*b*) An open door to ex-Ottoman Assyrians wishing to join their fellow countrymen in the sub-division quoted above.

(*c*) An investigation to be made by an authoritative Commission with a view to advising upon improvements of the Assyrian communities in Iraq.

(*d*) Appointment of Assyrian officials as originally recommended by the Frontier Commission of the League of Nations.

(*f*) The official language of the sub-liwa used along with Arabic should be Syriac.

To these claims the British Government replied that: "A special national status could not be given to the Assyrians without arousing demands for similar treatment from other racial, linguistic and religious minorities. The National unity of Iraq would thus be endangered.

"Further, unoccupied land does not exist in Iraq whereon the Assyrians could be settled as an autonomous community and, without compact settlement, administrative autonomy would be impracticable.

"In view of the difficulties attendant upon the settlement of the Assyrians already in Iraq, the United Kingdom Government does not feel justified in pressing the Iraqi Government to permit the immigration of large numbers of Assyrians.

"With regard to the request for an investigation into the condition of the Assyrian colonies, it is pointed out that a special committee has already been set up for this purpose . . . The question of registration of title is the subject of a scheme based on data supplied by an expert. The grant of title to Assyrian refugees on preferential terms would, however, provoke resentment among the other inhabitants.

"The request that Syriac should be recognised as the official language is inacceptable for similar reasons and, moreover, ignores the provisions of the Local Language law.

Finally, the Permanent Mandates Commission reached the following conclusion:

". . . draws the Council's special attention to the great importance, both for the Assyrians themselves and for Iraq, of providing the Assyrians with opportunities for settlement in a *homogeneous group* which would be in keeping with their traditions and would satisfy their economic needs.

For the rest, it considers, for the reasons stated in its Rapporteur's conclusions, that there is no need for it to submit to the Council any other special recommendation in regard to those petitions."

Assyrians' critical position recognised.

34. The conclusions reached by the Rapporteur were these:

" . . . there arises a definite impression that this community is dissatisfied with its present lot and profoundly uneasy as to its future.

"They are encamped there in conditions which, in most cases, are precarious and miserable; they are "refugees". In fact, these mountaineers have been settled in districts consistings of marshy and unhealthy plains, or dispersed in small groups or families in the midst of the Kurdish or Arab population.

"In the petitions which the Commission has had to deal with at its previous sessions, we find an expression of the feeling of insecurity inspired in the Assyrians, not only by the climate, with the casualties which it causes in their ranks, by the sterility of the land which has been assigned to them and by the precariousness of their rights to cultivate the soil, but *especially by the scattering of their community among populations of other races.*

"It is this latter circumstance which explains these individual acts of violence, these attacks against persons and property which the Assyrians have constantly complained of, and which they fear—since the cessation of British control has appeared imminent—will be multiplied to the point of making the conditions of existence of their community definitely intolerable.

"The root cause of the state of unrest revealed by the petitions we are dealing with resides in the fact that it has not yet been possible to collect the Assyrians of Iraq into a *homogeneous group* in a region suitable to their needs.

"It has not been proved to the satisfaction of an impartial observer that lands combining the requisite conditions for the settlement of the Assyrians in a homogeneous group *do* not exist in Iraq,

"There is here a situation worthy of engaging the League's attention. It concerns the very existence of a race whose glorious past goes back to the earliest history, and it also concerns the future of Iraq. The League has followed the progress accomplished by this young State, and has consecrated its political emancipation; any factor which may hamper its peaceful and harmonious development cannot leave the League indifferent."

CHAPTER FIVE

The Assyrian settlement in Iraq.

The settlement of the Assyrians in Iraq will necessarily have to be divided into three main periods:

(1) 1920-1925.
(2) 1925-1932.
(3) 1932-1933.

First period 1920-1925.

Assyrians unanimous to return to Hakkiari.

35. Ever since the Assyrians entered Iraq in 1918, they on no occasion expressed a desire to remain in that country. Their one and only one desire was that they should be returned to their original homes in Turkey or that arrangements be made that they emigrate from Iraq. If neither of these were possible, they desired to remain in Iraq under such conditions as would preserve their existence as a people, as they have been living before the war.

The suggested "Assyrian enclave".

36. Sir Percy Cox, on page 102 of his report on the administration of Iraq for period October, 1920-March 1922 states:
"Various schemes for settling the Assyrians had been mooted; and the most promising had been their suggested settlement in an enclave in the district of Amadiyah. This had been approved by Col. A.T. Wilson and by Colonel Leachman, political officer of Mosul. It was welcome to at least a great part of the people, and the Assyrian battalion raised among them to serve in Kurdistan (which did good service in the 1919 campaign) had indeed taken some rather drastic steps towards clearing the country. The

Home Government, however, was unable to come to a decision on the point until the British troops had been withdrawn from the country and the project rendered impracticable.

"The scheme had therefore to be dropped.

"The Assyrian refugees were divided into two main bodies, the Persian subjects, who were the plainsmen of Urumiyah, and the Turkish subjects, the mountaineers of Hakkiari. Both were clear as to what they wanted, and both wanted the same thing, viz., return to their own homes, and settlement there under British protection."

The Assyrians were unanimous in their determination to return to their homes in Turkey, and had the scheme of Sir Arnold Wilson's "Assyrian enclave" been carried out, the present massacre would have been out of the question, and the Assyrians would by now have become a quite prosperous and self-supporting people. This was not to be.

Assyrians used against Kurds, Turks and Arabs.

37. At a time when Assyrian levies were being raised by the British military and civil authorities on the strict understanding that this move was intended for the reoccupation of their homes in Turkey, these levies were used against:

(*a*) The Kurds
(*b*) The Turks and
(*c*) The Arabs who all aimed at undermining British authority in Iraq.

The Assyrians were used as a punitive force against the Kurds through whose territory they had to pass before reaching their homes, and against the Turks under whose reaching their homes, and against the Turks under whose zone of influence the "promised homes" were situated.

Turkish invasion of Mosul stopped.

38. Sir Percy Cox, in his report quoted above, makes the following statement:

"In justice to the Assyrians it must be added that during the first three months of this year, when a Turkish attack was always a possibility, they have proved their strategic value on the Iraq frontier. In March, over 2,000 enlisted in the Levies within three weeks. It is far from improbable that this instant response on the part of a people whose qualities as fighting men are renowned was the main reason which induced the Kemalists to abandon their projected attack. Led by British officers, they are a native force second to none. Their quickness in picking up discipline and their mettle in battle has surprised and delighted all who have been concerned with them."

This is typical of the services, not without losses to the Assyrians, which they have rendered to Iraq whilst Britain was occupied in laying down its foundations and arming it with authority and weapons which were used against its benefactors.

Repatriation of the Assyrians fails.

39. In 1919, the repatriation of the Assyrians to their original homes was begun. British officers were attached to the main Assyrian force, but partly due to defective organization and partly to bad weather, the scheme did not succeed.

Tiyari and Tkhuma tribes occupy Hakkiari.

40. In 1920, the two Assyrian tribes of Tiyari and Tkhuma returned to Hakkiari on their own initiative and actually occupied the territory over which the Turks had not yet established their authority.

British officer's visits arouse Turkish animosity.

41. Captain McNearnie and other recruiting British officers visited them in 1921 and succeeded in raising a considerable force among their numbers. These men were used by the British against the Turks, a fact which aroused Turkish animosity against the Assyrians.

As approximately 70 % of the Assyrian Young men were in the levies, and as the Turks were able by the year 1923 to mass large forces, the Assyrians in Hakkiari were stampeded out for they were no longer able to hold their own against the overwhelming Turkish regular forces fully equipped with all arms. The Assyrians were therefore compelled to retire to Iraq and their only and final chance of living peacefully in their ancestral homes was lost for ever.

It should be recorded that during the fight which ensued between the Turks and the Assyrians before the latter's retreat to Iraq, the Turks, despite the armed resistance offered them, captured 150 Assyrians, escorted them to the Iraqi frontier without molesting them.

Second period 1925-1932.

The reader will have seen how the Assyrians were used as a military force for a period of six years continuously under promises which were never fulfilled.

Sir Percy Cox' negotiations fail.

42. It was under those disturbing circumstances that Sir Percy Cox was instructed by the British Government in 1924 to claim at Constantinople the Hakkiari mountains with the ostensible idea of settling the Assyrians. The claim was flatly refused by the Turks as they well knew that the idea lying behind the demand was:

(*a*) To create a buffer State between Iraq and Turkey and

(*b*) To keep the Turks remote from Mosul as far as possible.

The British Government and certain British politicians blame the League of Nations for having allowed the Turks to retain Hakkiari. Well-informed people know that that was not so. If the Assyrians had been left alone, they could have somehow come to terms with the Turks whom the Assyrians understood and who understood them.

The "Z" plan.

43. Sir Percy Cox' negotiations alluded to above having failed, the British authorities launched upon a settlement scheme within the Mosul Wilayet which was now assigned to Iraq. The scheme was known as "the Z plan" which was to plant the Assyrians throughout Kurdistan from Dashta Baraz Gair bordering the Persian territory, right through the heart of Kurdistan and on to the north of Amadiyah, thus enabling Iraq to maintain a balance of power between herself and the Kurds who much resent the Arab régime. Moreover, in the plan the Assyrians were considered as an asset to Iraq should there be an external aggression.

Southern Kurdistan has never been tranquil, and the numerous Kurdish revolts to overthrow the Arab rule are well known to those interested in the affairs of Iraq and need not be repeated.

Assyrians levies garrison Kurdistan.

44. In Sulaimaniyah, Rowanduz, Rania and other parts of Kurdistan, Assyrian levies were stationed to keep in check the activities of the famous Kurdish leader, Shaikh Mahmud Barzanji. Amadiyah and Billeh were garrisoned by Assyrian levies. The latter garrison was to keep in order the Kurdish leader Shaikh Ahmad of Barzan who disregarded the authority of Iraq and administered an area of his own independently until 1932, when he was subdued by British aeroplanes to clear the "ugly atmosphere" of Kurdistan preparatory to Iraq's admission to the League of Nations. Captain Mumford for several years British Intelligence Officer and who is an authority on this subject has made it known that "The mandatory Power had to employ time—delayed bombs to subdue the Shaikh".

Nevertheless, the effects of "The Z plan" were disastrous to the Assyrians. The object for which it was drawn up could not have been otherwise. The scheme did not take into consideration the safety or the health of the Assyrians and only regarded the reasons which mooted it.

In certain districts, malaria and other diseases played havoc with the Assyrians as those regions fell within the "Z plan". The diseases were due to swampy areas and no prophylactic measures were taken to improve the situation. Malaria in those parts is not due to rice cultivation as the British government maintains. There are many districts inhabited by Assyrians where the effect of malaria or other diseases is not felt, although the settlers grow rice. In the districts of Nahla and Khalil kan, for instance, where in the Latter place no rice is grown, the death roll at times reached 95%, especially among children.

British officers and Americans have testified to this.

Third period 1932-33.

Arrival of Major D. B. Thomson in Iraq.

45. Such was the health of the Assyrians and their conditions generally when Major D. B. Thomson reached Iraq in June 1933 to settle the Assyrians in accordance with a resolution of the League of Nations.

Iraq was now independent and Thomson had no executive powers. The first signs of his activities tended to show that he was there to execute what Baghdad dictated to him. The Iraqi demagogues, the press and parliament objected to the settlement of the Assyrians. An intensive but perversive propaganda was set on foot. This had actually commenced some six months earlier and on Thomson's arrival the situation was tense. The future of the Assyrians was now in the hands of the same people against whom they fought side by side with the English in 1920 to maintain the latter's authority in the early days of the occupation.

The Iraq Government, as was anticipated, employed methods to cause dissension among the Assyrians, taking on its side certain individuals with whom Thomson was instructed to carry out Iraq's policy.

Coercive measures become acute.

46. Recognised Assyrian leaders were ignored and replaced by unpopular individuals. Coercive measures were taken against others under various pretexts and life was made desperate. Thomson's plan which he placed before the Assyrians covered the Dashtazi area, noted for malaria but within the "Z plan", politically detrimental to the interests of the Assyrians. The proposed area could have hardly accommodated 150 families. This is all the mandatory Power could do for the Assyrians. She persisted in using them for fifteen years and finally she told them:

"This is all that I can repay you. You must agree to be absorbed in the body politic of Iraq (which in practice meant that they should still remain homeless), must forget your language, traditions and customs and remain a disunited people for definite purposes."

"Even in your personal affairs, the Iraq Government must dominate."

Distribution of Assyrian population.

47. When Thomson came forward with his unsound settlement project, the distribution of the Assyrian population in Iraq was as follows:

	Settled Assyrians	Unsettled Assyrians
Mountaineers	17,270	
Mountaineers		14,000
Urumians		4,500
Others (such as those in Basra, Baquban, Ramadi, Kirkuk, etc.).		1,230
	17,270	19,730
Grand total	37,000	

CHAPTER SIX

The Patriarch's "Temporal Power".

Much harmful propaganda has been made in the Press regarding the "Patriarch's Temporal Power", a power which the Patriarch has been accused of having claimed. The object of such perversive propaganda has been to mislead public opinion by detracting its attention from the main issue.

Why did Assyrian recognise their Patriarch as Temporal Leader.

48. It is an indisputable fact, as history bears it out, that the Assyrians in order to prevent evil elements from penetrating through them thus wrecking their long established organization, and in order to preserve their existence as an entity, recognised their Patriarch as the Supreme Head of the Millet[1]!

This long-established rule was preserved intact for many centuries before and during the Turkish domination, and was recognised by the Sassanite Kings, the Caliphs, the Moghul khans and the Ottoman Sultans, until the entry of the Assyrians into Iraq in 1918 when it was no longer considered necessary.

When did the Patriarch practice Temporal Power.

49. The only time when the Patriarch practiced the "so-called temporal power" was when he was requested to do so by the British High Commissioners, particularly Sir Francis Humphrys who requested him to intervene between the mandatory Power and the Assyrians in times of difficulty. (See Mar Shimun's report dated October 8th, 1933, circulated by the League of Nations' secretariat to the members of the League Council document No. C.625. 1933.I.)

Major Wilson recommends detention of Patriarch, Lady Surma and Yaku Malik Ismail.

50. Since the formation of the provisional Arab Government in Iraq in 1920, and until the deportation of the Patriarch in August 1933, he applied for no temporal power either in writing or orally, either to the mandatory Power or to the Iraq Government. On the other hand, Major W.C.F.A. Wilson, administrative inspector, Mosul wrote to Baghdad on 10th May, 1933, as follows[1]:

"Ask Mar Shimun to come to Baghdad to discuss matters with the Government. Detention to follow forthwith. This should eliminate the danger of seeing Mar Shimun installed in his summer residence at Sar Amadiyah, the consequence of such a move will be against the interests of the Iraqi case.

"In order to break up the influence of the Patriarchal family, the Iraqi Government would be well advised in increasing immediately (from 6 to 8) of the Assyrian police inspectors.

"Immediate promotion of Christian officers having taken part in the campaign of the Iraq army against Shaikh Barzan.

"Lady Surma and Captain Yaku have undertaken a strong anti-government propaganda amongst the Kurdish tribes.

"It is urgently needed to invite these two persons to come to Baghdad where they should be detained and kept under control.

"Make pressure on the Patriarch to sign an official document recognising the suppression of his temporal power.

"Iraq government runs the risk of seeing the Assyrians proposing a scheme on lands near or bordering the Syrian frontier. All necessary steps should be taken to oblige the Patriarchal family to accept the Dashtazi region."

Removal of the Patriarch to Baghdad.

51. The Patriarch was taken to Baghdad under false pretences, and on May 28th, the Minister of Interior notified him (No. s/1104) that "Government could not invest him with any temporal power" just as if he had applied for such a power. The Patriarch was thereafter asked to sign

a document that he would not obstruct the task of Major D.B. Thomson who was to come to Iraq for purposes of settlement and that he will always and in every way remain as one of the most faithful subjects of His Majesty the Great King[1].

No reason or proof in support of such an attitude either in regard to obstructiveness in settlement or of disloyalty were put forward by the Minister of Interior despite the request of, and facts brought by the Patriarch to the contrary.

However, to avert the evil consequences which the Government aimed at, the Patriarch gave assurances that he would do his best to help Major Thomson and expressed in no uncertain terms his loyalty to the King.

However short-sighted the Ministers of the Iraq Government were to be, they should have realised that the illegal detention and mal-treatment of the Patriarch was only adding to the list of cases of oppression, now so common in Mosul, which would not be tolerated by the Assyrians, and would only promote suspicion and create chaos and tension resulting in disaster.

Can it be said that the Iraq government had any other idea in view?

CHAPTER SEVEN

The forced exodus to Syria.

Major Thomson a complete failure.

52. Thomson's two previous meetings and his personal tours of Assyrian settlements showed the impracticability of his scheme, unless modified, but unfortunately he persisted in it until on the 10th and 11th of July 1933 two more meetings, attended by Assyrian leaders to hear the Iraq Government's ultimatum, were held in the office of Mutasarrif, Mosul, Khalil 'Azmi.

Speech of Mutasarrif, Mosul.

53. During the meeting of July 10th, the Arab acting Mutasarrif explained the Iraq Government's policy and finally said:

"It is in the interest of Assyrians who decide to reside in Iraq to obtain nationality certificates, for the Iraq Government cannot allot lands to those who do not consider themselves Iraqis; such people cannot expect to attain private or government positions without it."

Iraq nationality papers

54. The idea behind the suggestion to obtain Iraqi nationality papers *before* allotment of land was made to induce the Assyrians to obtain such papers and to inform the League of Nations (even if the large majority of the Assyrians remained homeless) that the Assyrians have been settled and in proof thereof: "Here is a list of those who have obtained the nationality papers".

Ninety per cent of the Iraqi population have no nationality papers and few government officials, possess them. Moreover, the Assyrian people in Iraq were Iraqi nationals by virtue of those provisions of the Treaty of Lausanne which are reproduced in the Iraqi Nationality Law.

Col. Stafford notifies Assyrians to find a new home.

55. The acting Mutasarrif then asked his British Adviser, Colonel R.S. Stafford, to explain his points of view, particularly those of the neighbouring countries, should the Assyrians decide to leave Iraq. He said:

"What has impressed me most has been the lack of contact between Assyrians and the government officials. They appear until quite recently to have considered themselves as being foreigners living in a strange land. I want all you Assyrian leaders who are present to-day to realise once and for all that this is an intolerable situation and one which must end. There is no middle path . . . or they must be prepared to leave the country. As regards the second alternative which I have mentioned, that of leaving Iraq. The Iraq government has undertaken to grant every facility to those Assyrians who wish to leave Iraq. That is to say that no one who wishes to go will be prevented from so doing. But the Iraq government is in no way responsible for finding a place outside Iraq for Assyrians to go to. It is up to Assyrians themselves to make such arrangements, both as regards to obtaining approval from the government of the country in which they wish to settle and as regards the expenses of transport.

"*Turkey*. There is not the slightest chance of the Turkish government modifying its present attitude towards Assyrians. It will not accept them at any price.

"*Persia*. The Persian Government has said that it would accept small groups of Assyrians but the conditions offered are hard (i) all arms to be surrendered. (ii) settlement not to be in one place but in very widely separated places. (iii) no rights in the land to be given. (iv) no financial assistance to be given.

"*Syria*. As you are aware the French authorities in Syria already have the problem of the Armenian refugees. They have no land to offer Assyrians. It is true that young Assyrians might be able to obtain employment in the French Colonial armies, but let me tell you that such service is hard in the extreme. Nor would there be any future for such men in Syria, while the Iraq Government would naturally be unwilling to allow their return to Iraq. In view of the present economic crisis it is not to be expected that any country in the world would welcome Assyrian emigrants. Everyone understands and regrets the difficulties and the sufferings of the Assyrians. The Iraq Government which is responsible for neither is going to do its best to help. If you wish to flourish, you must be prepared to work hard.

"The acting Mutasarrif has dealt fully with the question of the Mar Shimun; I need only remark that what he has said is self evident truth and one which requires no explanation. In conclusion I have to say that the time has now arrived for you to decide once and for all whether you are going to stay in Iraq or not."

The Assyrians did their utmost to keep on friendly terms and serve the Iraq Government loyally, but the past British policy was always a barrier between the two.

When the Assyrians made their own arrangements to find a new home, they were stopped by diplomatic pressure and force of arms. The Iraqi officials told the Assyrians that the Government would bear their transport expenses up to the frontier.

Lord Noel-Buxton and the French.

56. As regards the diplomatic pressure, the following statement made by Lord Noel-Buxton on 28th November, 1933, in the House of Lords is worth while recording:

"It has been asserted by people of weight that when the Assyrians crossed into Syria, we used influence with the French Government to prevent their staying in Syria."

Major Thomson's speech.

57. Following Mutasarrif and Stafford's speeches to the Assyrians, Major Thomson made the following announcement: "Make up your minds once and for all that you must settle in Iraq. No other country will offer you the terms and conditions that you are being given by the Iraq Government. Decide to make the best of it without further delay."

The speeches made left no doubt in the minds of the Assyrians that they were not wanted in Iraq. It was also quite evident that the only door open to them, under the circumstances, was Syria where their compatriots were living in peace for some years now.

First Assyrian group leave for Syria

58. On the night of 14-15 July, 1933, a large group of Assyrians headed by representative leaders of all Assyrian tribes left Iraq peacefully and reached Syrian frontier.

The letter of July 23rd.

59. On July 23rd, they informed the Minister of Interior at Baghdad in writing that they had left Iraq as a result of the meetings held at Mosul on 10th and 11th July and requested him not to molest their families and other Assyrians wishing to join them. It must be remembered that the Assyrians before reaching the Syrian border had to march over a hundred miles and their spirit can be judged by the fact that not a single incident took place.

Instead of honouring its pledges, the Iraq Government mobilized two thirds of its army, practically all its police force, recruited some 1,500 irregular police in Mosul liwa, and began harassing the Assyrians.

The Anglo-French discussions in Paris and the Franco-Iraqi negotiations on the frontier took place with a view to:

(*a*) Disarm the Assyrians and
(*b*) Return them to Iraq.

Had the French authorities complied with this request, the total massacre in cold blood of those who took shelter under the French Flag was a certainty as the subsequent events will show.

The situation of those in Iraq became alarming. They were prevented in spite of what they were given to understand at the Mosul meeting from joining their compatriots and this forcible prevention did not pass without incidents.

Iraqi Ministers remove their headquarters to Mosul preparatory to massacre.

60. Before the actual fight of August 4th, preparations were being made with the full knowledge of the Iraqi cabinet to massacre all Assyrians remaining in Iraq. Hikmat Sulaiman, Minister of Interior, Sabih Najib, Director General of Police, and the Minister for War changed their headquarters from Baghdad to Mosul, an unprecedented move in all former Kurdish armed revolutions.

The Holy war.

61. In Parliament and in Senate, inflammatory speeches against the Assyrians were made in the nature of a Holy War. In the Mosques, meetings headed by Members of Parliament were held. Deputies volunteered to take

up arms, to proceed to Mosul and to fight the Assyrians. All Arab classes were called by the Government organs, such as newspapers and others, to join in the Holy War. Non-compliance meant treachery.

Assyrians attacked in the river Faish-khabur.

62. On June 29th, long before the exodus to Syria, the Patriarch protested to twelve Foreign Embassies, including that of Great Britain (sending the original protest to the Minister of Interior). From the Minister of Interior he received no reply and the British Embassy was silent. Because of the latter's protest, however, certain Iraqi newspapers, which had during this period published two articles only considered prejudicial to British interests, were suppressed.

The Patriarch's protest of June 29th, 1933.

63. Finally those in Syria were assured by Iraq that no harm would come to them if they returned and surrendered their arms. On this assurance and more particularly to avoid any bloodshed in Mosul, they agreed to do so and started crossing river Faishkhabour, the frontier river which divides Syria and Iraq. The Iraq army was strongly entrenched and was already commanding all the strategic points in the area. No sooner did a group of Assyrians reach the middle of the river than an Iraqi aeroplane flew over and after giving a signal, a terrific fire of all arms was opened on them. Assyrians on the river shore and those in the river, bearing in mind the safety of their families, did not retaliate. Renewed signals of surrender in the form of white flags were made but the only response the Assyrians received from the enemy was an intense fire. Under the circumstances, retaliation was the only remedy, especially when they saw that their dead and wounded were increasing rapidly. The Assyrians led by their respective chiefs namely, Yaku and Shlaimun Malik Ismail, Malik Loko and David of Tkhuma and others went to their rescue. They split their force in two groups. Yaku surprised the enemy from the rear whilst Malik Loko launched a frontal attack dislocating the Iraq army from Baikhir hill thus rescuing their comrades.

Iraqi aeroplane kills 3 officers.

64. The fight lasted all the night of 4-5 August; the Iraq army retreating leaving behind much ammunition and other war materials, which was

subsequently blown up by an Iraqi aeroplane. Three of their own officers who were captured by the Assyrians and detained in a tent were killed by the explosion. The Iraq Government, to further arouse Arab fanaticism, falsely accused the Assyrians of having killed and mutilated the bodies of these officers.

The Assyrian casualties were:

Killed: 8. Wounded: 15.

Before ending this chapter, it is necessary to quote some extracts from a letter dated July 31st, 1933, from the Rev. Dr. John B. Panfil (American) of the Episcopal Mission in Mosul to give the reader a clear view of the true facts-coming as they are from a disinterested observer.

Rev. Dr. John B. Panfil's testimony.

65. "The Assyrians who left Iraq represent 15,000 persons counting their families; thousands more are waiting for an opening in the military belt, to leave. The villages north of Mosul are deserted, rice fields left to dry, sheep abandoned in the hands of servants. It can be said that this third exodus of the Assyrians since the war, is general.

"The reasons for this desperate move are many. The Assyrians were promised and hoped for a special treatment if they were to remain in Iraq. They joined their little forces with the Allies and fought on the side of the British army in Persia and Iraq. The long and bitter experience of the past has proved to them that they can not live in the villages of Kurds without a special arrangement: they knew that they can not expect much assistance from a Moslem Government in case of difficulty. They knew that in the last incident of Yaco, the Government actually armed the Kurds against them. They were told that they will have to give up their arms before anybody else.

"The Government appointed five new leaders from different tribes, gave positions and salaries to the opposers of the Patriarch, and favoured specially the Presbyterian Assyrians. A regular campaign against the Patriarchal authority was conducted in the villages by the Government officials. Those friendly disposed toward the Patriarch were ill-treated, arrested and persecuted in many ways. The chiefs of the villages were called again and again under different pretexts and told to betray Mar Shimun. The house of the Patriarch was watched and he was warned not to hold any meetings.

"The Assyrians could not accept new leaders; could not resign themselves to be persecuted unjustly; could not drop so abruptly their allegiance to their Patriarch. The villages began to boil with unrest.

"The meeting of July 10th, gathered by the Government, blasted the last hope of the Assyrians, regarding their settlement. The Government made it clear to them that only a fraction of them will be settled in Dashta Zeh and others will have to stay where they are. Major Thomson, the settlement officer, seemed to be bound to the Government's policy. The great question of settlement as cherished in the minds of the Assyrians, was reduced to a mere shifting of some 600 families from one place to another.

"The offensive remarks about the Assyrians in the Parliament, made it clear to them that they are unwanted in Iraq. The Arabic press by publishing articles against the Assyrians, created an hostile feeling among the local population. The publishing in the American Press, of the article, known to you, by Rev. Cumberland, and its translation in the Arabic papers, filled the hearts of the Assyrians with discouragement. These and other of longer standinga-causes, forced the Assyrians, to the desperate move of leaving Iraq.

"Those who left will not return to Iraq. If forced they will fight, try to go to Turkey or disperse in the mountains. If France accepts them, all others will slowly follow. The Assyrians know now that the Government does not want them and that the general public hates them. They were ready last December to go to Persia but they preferred to give themselves up to France, which retains still the prestige of protecting the oppressed in the East. In Syria they will know that they will have no rights to ask for privileges or special treatment, that they will have to give up their arms: but they are ready for that in order to be able to cultivate their grounds and pasture their cattle in peace. Still this is a slip in the British policy in the East, which will be judged severely in the annals of future history."

———

CHAPTER EIGHT

The massacre.

Bakr Sidqy was the Arab area commandant, Mosul. He and the local officials, no doubt in league with Baghdad, had planned the massacre for the month of May 1933.

The stone case.

66. On May 7th, an Arab officer living next door to the Patriarchate complained that stones were thrown into his house. The Patriarchal House was accused and the accusation was extended to other Assyrians. The Police took the matter up and stated, as a result of their investigations, that they failed to know the source of the stones.

By the 15th May, the whole quarter was vacated by the Arab officers living there, including Bakr Sidqy, and other officials. The army occupied all the strategic points around the town of Mosul. On the 13th, the Patriarch met the Mutasarrif to discuss the situation with him. He stated that he himself did not know what the military arrangements were for and recommended that the Patriarch should meet Bakr Sidqi. The Mutasarrif telephoned to Bakr Sidqy who replied that he was unable to see the Patriarch that day but would do so the following day. That day never came. On the 16th, the Assyrians in Mosul were asked to surrender their arms.

As Assyrian levies were also accused, the Air Vice-Marshal came from Baghdad and after holding a Commission of Enquiry and finding the falsehood of the accusation, the case was closed and thus the plot was averted. The accused Assyrians after being sent for trial were acquitted.

Removal of Assyrian police from Mosul.

67. In order to be able to carry on the plot successfully later, almost all the Assyrians in the Police force were transferred from Mosul to the south of Iraq.

After the battle of the 4/5th August, as already narrated, the Assyrians combatants returned to Syria where they now remain under French protection. The Assyrian Nation should never fail to express its gratitude for this act of humanity and justice which France has taken. The Iraq army returned to Mosul and right through its way began a systematic massacre, which commenced on August 7th when Qaimaqam Zakho Ahmad al Dibuni tortured to death forty-six Assyrians while the Iraq army executed any Assyrian it met on its way back. While this was going on, pamphlets signed by the Iraq government were dropped by British[1] and Iraqi aeroplanes asking the Assyrians to surrender their arms and that no harm would come to them. The fact that those leaflets were dropped by British aeroplanes as well gave the Assyrians an implicit assurance of their safety without which they would have hesitated in responding under the prevailing circumstances.

Inauguration of the massacre.

68. The wholesale massacre was officially inaugurated on the 11th of August. The massacre zone is 15/30 miles from Mosul which is linked up with telephone, telegraph and by other means of communication. The Minister of Interior, Hikmat Sulaiman, pretended that he only heard of the massacre on the 14th when orders to stop it were given as its object had already been fulfilled.

Arabs and certain Kurds were armed by the government and offered one pound for every Assyrian head. They were also told that all means employed against the Assyrians were lawful and Government would take no action against them.

Civil officials from Mosul joined in the massacre which was arranged as follows:

The Simel massacre.

69. Under pretext of giving police protection to the Assyrians, the inhabitants of eleven villages in the vicinity of Simel (the larger Assyrian village whose police post was beforehand reinforced) were summoned to the latter place for shelter from the tribesmen government had armed. Men, women and children hurried to the place of protection. After assuring them of the "good intentions" of the Government, they were disarmed by the police

authorities under instructions of Makki Sharbatti Qaimaqam[1] of Dohuk. The inoffensive population was indiscriminately massacred, men, women and children alike, with rifle, revolver and machine gun fire. In one room alone, *eighty-one* men from the Baz tribe, who had taken shelter with the named Goriyyil, were barbarously massacred. Priests were tortured and their bodies mutilated. Those who showed their *Iraqi nationality* papers were the first to be shot. Girls were raped and women violated and made to march naked before the Arab army commander. Holy books were used as fuel for burning girls. Children were run over by military cars. Pregnant women were bayonetted. Children were flung in the air and pierced on to the points of bayonets. Those who survived in the other villages were now exposed day and night to constant raids and acts of violence Forced conversion to Islam of men and women was the next process. Refusal was met with death.

65 villages, looted, destroyed or burnt.

70. *Sixty five* out of ninety five Assyrian villages and settlements were either sacked, destroyed or burnt to the ground. Even the settlements which existed from the year 1921 and who had no connection in any way with the trouble were wrecked and all property looted by Iraq army and tribesmen.

Assyrian villages in regions such as Kurai Gawana, Barwari Jairi and Sapna valley in Amadiyah qadha shared also the same fate after surrendering their arms in the same way as did the others.

In Dohuk, the town crier, under orders of the Arab Qaimaqam informed the public that anyone harbouring an Assyrian will be severely dealt with. Under the orders of this Qaimaqam alone, *five hundred Assyrians* who had handed in their *arms* following the official pamphlets dropped from air were killed round Dohuk.

Over 100 Assyrians were removed in lorries from their villages and Dohuk town and were killed by machine guns on the frontier area to show that they had fallen during the official engagement.

Dismissal of Assyrians from British employment.

71. In other parts of Iraq, the Assyrians in the British employment such as railways were dismissed as this was the desire of the Arabs, and those in the employ of the Petroleum Company were attacked by Arabs with several casualties.

British aeroplanes take photographs of horrible scenes.

72. No relief was afforded by the British authorities. The only thing the Royal Air Force, whose aerodromes the Assyrians were and are still guarding, did was to take photographs from air of scenes of horror, and after permission from the Iraq government, the Royal Air Force removed to Baghdad the remaining immediate families of the levies, some 189 persons.

All foreigners in the district affected were withdrawn about ten days before the massacre.

To give the reader a better knowledge of the atrocities, the following quotations must be recorded.

On November 28th, in the House of Lords, His Grace the Archbishop of Canterbury said:

" . . . I have already indicated to Your Lordships that it cannot fairly be described as a *rebellion*. It was a possibly misguided attempt on the part of these Assyrians to do what they understood from the Government they were at liberty to do, to go and find a new home if they could. And I ought to add—I ought to have done it at an earlier stage—that if they were asked to stay they could not but remember that at that very time there were outbreaks of the fiercest and most fanatical language in the Iraqi press and also in the Iraqi parliament which received no sort of check. Is it to be wondered at that they said plainly: "We are not wanted in Iraq, and if we can get the French to take us in Syria, let us go". In regard to the massacre he said:

"I have seen accounts of those who were present. I have heard that it was more shocking than anything it was seen during the war. And I have read a letter from an independent and trustworthy person in Iraq, by no means friendly to the Assyrians, who said that such an exhibition of savage fanaticism has probably seldom been seen. There is no question that it was done by the *Iraq army*. I do not know how far any orders had been issued by the Commander, Sidqy beg. It is enough to say that full credit for this was taken by the whole army. It was shortly afterwards received by acclamation in the streets of Baghdad, and Sidqy beg was promoted to Pasha."

Before the massacre the feeling in Iraq was anti-British. But afterwards the turn of Arab opinion can be judged by the following statement.

Mr. Ernest Main, who was sent to Iraq as the Daily Mail representative, and flew by the same aeroplane as did Sir Francis Humphrys who was recalled from his fishing expedition in Norway, speaking at the Royal Central Asian Society[1] said:

"Among the Arabs feeling appeared to swing round in favour of Britain. When I left Baghdad they were beginning to appreciate that they must depend on British support at Geneva, and the general feeling was much more definitely pro-British than when I arrived a month earlier."

The Assyrians massacred during August 1933 were 3,000.

Extracts from the following two reports written by two Presbyterian American Missionaries are further proofs of facts already narrated.

Report of Mr. Badeau.

Report of Mr. Badeau, American missionary.

73. "Official communiqués are usually very unsatisfactory sources of information, and those issued by the Iraq Government during the recent Assyrian troubles are no exception to the rule . . . So far the Government seem to have handled the situation fairly well-considering the character of the Arab officials and the traditional feud between the Kurds and Assyrians. But on the eleventh of August there occurred an incident for which there can be no excuse whatsoever. One can say that it was sheer, brutal savagery—a revision to the worst days of the Turkish treatment of the Armenians.

"Some miles from Dohuk there is (or was) an Assyrian village called Sumeil. It lies in the plain at the base of the Kurdish hill ranges, and near it are several other Assyrian villages. These villages did not belong to the dissafected group. Their men had not left to cross into Syria. Many of the villages were Iraqi citizens, and during the troubles had remained loyal to the Government. Altho the orders were to allow all loyal Assyrians to retain their arms, many of the villagers had given their's up to the police when the Government ordered the surrounding villagers to come to Sumeil where there was a police post and they could be protected. Then either the tenth of August or the morning of the eleventh, the remaining arms were collected so that the villages—even had it been rebellious—was incapable of any kind of resistance.

"This defenseless village, packed with refugees, was then systematically massacred. All of the men, with the exception of two or three who had gone to Dohuk were killed. The small Arab population of the town was untouched. Estimates of the number massacred vary from a minimum of three hundred and fifty to seven hundred. It is extremely difficult to get an accurate estimate at this time, as no impartial or European observer has been allowed in Sumeil. I suppose the truth will never be fully known, for the only people on the spot—the Iraq army—"do not choose" to tell, at least the truth.

"The Government communiqué issued in response to certain articles appearing in the English papers stated that if there had been a massacre (a fact which seemed dubious!) it was the work of the Arabs and Kurdish tribesmen who were looting. But the truth is that all the evidence points to the Iraq army itself, acting under definite orders. All the survivors testify that the killing was done by "men in blue shirts". It is obvious that the Arab never uses any shirt, and the Kurd does not use blue ones. The only section of the population wearing blue shirts is the Machine Gun Corps—so the massacre must have been at the hands of the forces sent there for "protection". At dusk the Arabs and Kurds did come in to loot, and they probably killed some of the wounded. But the Government claim that (if there was a massacre!) the Arabs and Kurds did the killing and the troops hurried there for the defense of the village cannot be accepted as anything but sheer and deliberate untruthfulness.

"The British Administrative Inspector had ordered the Cumberlands out of Dohuk on the sixth, and they came at once to Mosul.

" . . . On the sixteenth the Minister again requested that I confer with him, and suggested that all our missionaries be withdrawn from the Mosul district. He requested this action both as a precautionary measure of personal safety, and because the Iraq Foreign Office had sent him a strongly worded note protesting against alleged "Political activities" of Mr. Panfil and Mr. Cumberland. He feared that if a second protest was made the Government would request the people involved to leave the country and so in the interests of our work strongly advised temporary withdrawal.

"The rest of the missionaries remained in Baghdad, where they are at the present. Mr. Willoughby wanted to return on this coming Monday to Mosul, but the Minister after conference with the British Ambassador (who returned hurriedly from Scotland) had advised him to stay a few days longer until it is apparent what course of action the Iraq Government intends to take.

"I am much concerned about the accusation brought against Mr. Cumberland. The note used strong phrases in referring to his "philanthropic and religious work which is being used as a blind for political activities". It is understandable why the Iraq Government should suspect Mr. Panfil. He has been close to Mar Shimun and has on several occasions acted as a mediator between the Government and the Assyrians (at the Government's request, however). He gave bond for Yaku, the leader. But even these doubtful "political activities" cannot be attributed to Mr. Cumberland. His article about the Assyrians in the April "World Dominion" was *highly acclaimed* by the local press as an exoneration of Iraq's Assyrian policy, and several of the Arab Government *officials* have spoken to both him and me in *praise* of it. During these troubles (as well as long before) Mr. Cumberland used his influence to induce the Assyrians to become good Iraqis, and to trust the Government, and yet this is "political activity".

"As a matter of fact, we think that the real purpose back of the note was to clear all possible witnesses out of the troubled area . . . The Government does not want any contradictions or corrections of the *official reports*, or any witnesses who can tell what really happened. The note from the Foreign office came *directly* after the Sumeil massacre, from which I deduce that the occurences of that incident so embrassed the Government that they hurried all *impartial* onlookers out of the area.

"The Minister has promised to take the matter up with the Iraq Government as soon as the present fever heat of anti-Assyrian feeling has subsuded. Mr. Cumberland has tried to have an appointment with the Minister of Foreign Affairs, but the return of the *triumphant* Iraq army fresh from its *slaughters* has temporarily made it difficult. It will be hard to get the Government to retract its charges, and I am not sure that we ought to press for a formal restriction if doing so will only create ill will. When the troubles are over the Government will probably "forget" its charges and allow the Cumberlands to return without further protest.

"The Government probably used the growing Assyrian discontent as a counter-irritant to the Shia-Sunni trouble in lower Iraq. I have been told that had the Assyrian incident not occured there would have been a *Shia* outbreak in the South. When Faisal returned hurriedly from England this summer it was reported that the reason was the Shia discontent, rather than the Assyrian troubles. The Assyrian uprising made a splendid appeal to Iraqi patriotism against a foreign group, and *Moslem* prejudice against the *Christians*, and diverted attention from internal Moslem troubles.

"It was hardly fair to put much an involved and difficult problem as the Assyrian question into the hands of a new and *inexperienced* Government. It ought to have been settled by the British Government, before they relinquished their mandate. British precaution and British promises brought the Assyrians to this country, British policy should have provided for them.

"Its is difficult to play the prophet and forsee the future. There is at present, amongst the very nationalistic Government circles, definite *anti-British* and anti-Christian feeling. It would not be impossible that the present cabinet might force Faisal to relinquish his throne and set up a republic, destroying all British treaties. No one knows. But I think that within a fairly short time the situation will be clarified, and we will be able to return to our stations.

"Since all mail is being censored I am sending this by Miss Honse to Jerusalem. Please be extremely guarded in any reply you may make. As soon as the mails are once again reliable I will inform you.

"I am sending a copy of this to Dr. Cantine, and one to the Near East Christian Council's committee on Government and Missions."

Report of Mr. R.C. Cumberland.

1-2-231 Sinak.
Baghdad.
26th August 1933

Report of Mr. R. C. Cumberland, American missionary.

74. "On Sunday, 6th August, I received a telephone call from Col. Stafford, the Administrative Inspector in Mosul, asking me to bring my wife to Mosul, which I did that day. The Iraqi Foreign Minister wrote to our Minister Mr. Knabenshue, complaining of my political activities and requesting my removal from Dohuk. I might add that no specific charges were made and no evidence brought against me; and that up to the present I have not succeeded in getting an interview with the Foreign Minister. It seems to me obvious that Government does not want any foreign observer in the Dohuk district at present, rather than that it objects to any alleged political activities of mine. It is not surprising that the Government wishes to have the present situation concealed; it is not a pleasant sight . . . But I find it hard to be content here in Baghdad; I shall do my utmost to arrange to return to Dohuk as soon as possible.

"In the meantime it may be well for me to write as fully as possible regarding the situation; for a postal censorship is easily possible, and I shall probably refrain from writing some kinds of things.

"A very interesting chapter might be written, if all the materials were available, on real and supposed British promises to the Assyrians; they form at least a part of the basic of the defiance of the Iraqi Government which has brought things to their present pass . . . These Assyrians are described by Iraqi press dispatches as rebels and insurgents, but I do no think those words accurately describe them . . . This I know; all or nearly all of the Assyrian villages in the plain have been looted. Most of the looting was done by Arabs and Kurds; most of the killing was done by the *army*.

"The massacre at Semeil is known to you . . . having been told to come in from the surrounding villages for protection. They were all without arms, and were shot down in cold blood by the army. Such an exhibition of stark savagery and frenzied fanaticism has seldom been seen. In addition to this, I know not how many innocent people were taken from their homes in Dohuk, while I was there, and have not been seen since. The Simeil massacres and similar events have gone far to destroy the confidence of the Assyrians and of other minority groups, especially Christians, in the good faith of the Government. There seems not to be the personal *integrity* in the Government services to form a *stable* administration. To be sure, we as Americans are not in position to throw stones; but the objective fact remains that *corruption* is the rule rather than the exception in this country, and that it is not condemned by any body of public opinion that is strong enough to check it. The outlook is not bright; the necessity for the work we are here to do is all the more evident.

"What course Government will take, I cannot forecast. I am sorry that that for the present they have chosen to deny the facts of the Smeil massacre; it does no good. One of the most discouraging features of the situation is the strong feeling, especially in Mosul, against all Assyrians, whether loyal to Government or not. Many Assyrians employed in all kinds of work are being dismissed these days, for no reason other than that they are Assyrians.

"At Semeil was proved what fanatical Islam and irresponsible Government are capable of, and it will not soon be forgotten . . . I should not doubt that a wise solution would be reached. But this will go to London and Geneva, where there cannot be such a background of understanding, and where France will have a hand in it, on account of the connection with Syria. I have a profound distrust of French colonial policy. In spite of Iraqi denials, the main features of the facts will be known, and they cannot be entirely overlooked. Protests ought to be made. But I do not think that armed intervention would have a reaction in this country opposite to that desired, unless the League or some country appointed by it is ready to step in and establish a complete foreign administration.

"Mr. Badeau's letter to Dr. Chamberlain will give you a digest of facts, and I understand that Mr. Willoughby has also *written* . . .

"I am furnishing this a few minutes before Miss Honse sets out on her homeward journey, taking it with her to avoid the postal censor."

———————

CHAPTER NINE

The Patriarch's position vis-a-vis the massacre

The Patriarch cut off from Assyrians in Mosul.

75. On May 22nd, 1933, the Patriarch was removed to Baghdad under false pretences and stayed at the Young Men Christian Association which was subsequently surrounded by a cordon of plain clothes men. His Outward and Inward correspondence was tampered with and confiscated. He was totally cut off from the Assyrians in the Mosul Liwa.

In June, he discussed the settlement question with Major Thomson and found him persistent in the Iraq Government policy which was doomed to failure so long as it remained inimical towards the Assyrians.

Assyrian requests to set Patriarch free ignored.

76. The written demands of the Assyrian chiefs to set the Patriarch free were ignored by the Government. Simultaneously with this, the Arab Minister of Interior asked the Patriarch not to interfere in the settlement which he said the "Government classified as temporal question". On the other hand, Thomson and the British Advisers in the service of the same Minister asked the Patriarch to cooperate. The Patriarch was unable to reconcile these contradictory demands and informed those concerned accordingly.

Thomson discusses settlemend with levies.

77. In Mosul, Thomson had a meeting with the Assyrian levies who refused to discuss with him the settlement scheme and they informed him that they were under a pledge not to interfere in politics. He replied that "Land settlement did not come under that heading".

British Ambassador undertakes stop massacre.

78. The first news of the massacre were conveyed to the Patriarch by the Assyrian levies who were hurriedly removed from Sar Amadiyah where they were guarding the British summer camp, to Baghdad. They were unable to give details because they were prevented from seeing the actual conditions. In August, the Patriarch had the alarming news radiographed to the League of Nations and to various Heads of European Nations. The British ambassador told the Patriarch that there was no likelihood of the massacre being stopped unless he left Iraq. The Patriarch consented to do so after receiving an assurance that:

(*a*) The massacre would be stopped and
(*b*) The Air Vice-Marshal would go up to Mosul and establish a camp for the destitute.

The British ambassador also told the Patriarch that after leaving Iraq, he would be free to place the case of his people before the League of Nations.

Air Vice-Marshal prevented from establishing refugee camp.

79. The plan of the wholesale massacre ended on 14th of August but individual murders continued long after the Patriarch left Iraq and the Air Vice-Marshal, squadron leader Reed (purposely brought from Palestine) and Captain Baddiley of the Assyrian levies proceeded as far as Mosul where they were prevented by the Iraqi authorities from going any farther.

Patriarch deported on August 18th.

80. On August 15th, an emergency law for the deportation of the Patriarch was passed and his Iraqi nationality annulled with the approval of the British Embassy.
Article 7 of the constitutional law of Iraq lays down.
"Torture and the deportation of Iraqis from the Kingdom of Iraq are absolutely forbidden"
On August 18th, the emergency law was enforced and the Patriarch was removed by the British air force from the Hinaidi aerodrome to Cyprus via Palestine by air.

Assyrian chiefs banished.

81. Meanwhile, other Assyrian chiefs were banished from their homes in Mosul to the lower Euphrates.

Issue of laissez-passer conditional.

82. As soon as the Patriarch arrived in Cyprus on August 21st, he applied to the Governor for permission to proceed to Geneva to plead the cause of his people. The matter was referred to London. A laissez-passer was not granted to the Patriarch, however, until the 28th day of September, and *not* before he gave the following undertaking to the Government of Cyprus.

"In pursuance of the correspondence, noted in the margin hereof, between myself and the acting colonial secretary, Cyprus, a copy of which is annexed hereto, I, the undersigned Mar Shimun, Patriarch of the Nestorians (Assyrians), hereby undertake that I will not while in the United Kingdom indulge in any public activity in the nature of propaganda."

On 22nd September, the Patriarch wrote to the Acting colonial secretary suggesting to him that the undertaking should be modified in the following form and this was inacceptable;

" . . . I also realize that whilst in the United Kingdom, I am not permitted by His Britannic Majesty's Government to indulge in any public activity in the nature of propaganda, *other than by normal courses.*"

The Patriarch left Cyprus and arrived in Geneva on October 4th, and had only nine days during which time he had to prepare the case of his people.

The Assyrians in general, in Iraq and outside such as America and other places, despite their poverty have generously contributed towards the expenses of the Patriarch in representing their case to the League of Nations and the public opinion.

CHAPTER TEN

The present Assyrian situation in Iraq.

The destitute in Dohuk after the massacre.

83. It was 20 days after the "official massacre" that thousands of old men, women and children who were left without any young male relatives were handed over to Thomson. During this interval, they were accommodated in a khan[1] without any roof in Dohuk, and the police whose duty was to look after them, selected the prettiest of women in the evenings and returned them at dawn. Many perished from the heat of the day, famine, and terror. An Assyrian who had lost six family members was made, on the point of revolver, to sign a document to the effect *"that he was happy in Iraq"*.

The destitute and helpless were exposed to acts of violence and terrorism.

The Mosul camp.

84. A camp in Mosul was opened to receive the panic-stricken population. One of the members of the relief committee was Faiq beg, director of Tapu[2], who is proud of having taken an active part in the massacre. Assyrian individuals in the employment of the Iraq government were instructed to pursuade the victims of the massacre to say that the *Kurds*, and not the Iraq army, were those who committed the atrocities.

The Iraq Government was charged with the task of looking after the refugees. Major Thomson has reported that the conditions of the refugees is "good". But in his report for period ending November 30th, 1933, he gives the following account of the assistance rendered.

"By August 30th, there were in the Mosul camp 1,294 women and children.

"By September 14th, the total number was 1563.

"By the end of November, there were 1,536 persons.

"Between September 14th and November 30th, 213 were admitted and 189 either removed by their relatives or the Royal air force.

"Though the camp is primarily for destitute women and children, it was found necessary to admit some 70 men, who were destitute through blindness, paralysis, loss of limbs or old age."

27 orphan boys had no relatives left at all.

548 persons were accommodated in 3 houses in all containing 24 rooms or some 23 persons in each room. The maximum that a room can normally accommodate is 8 persons.

Until the 20th of October, there was an English doctor deputed by the Air Vice-Marshal to afford medical relief to the refugees.

Through carelessness, poor food, severe cold and insufficient clothing, the destitute have suffered from diphtheria, malaria, coughs and other malady.

Thomson states that during the period 30th August to 30th November, there have been 70 deaths among the children. The statistics sent to the Patriarch show that the death roll among the children alone was 95.

Thomson concludes his report by saying:

"The sum actually spent on the running of the camp does not exceed 200 Iraqi dinars (Pounds) per week. This amount covers food, milk, rent of the houses, tents, pay of staff, electric light and minor incidental expenses."

The 200 dinars is equivalent to 3,200 Swiss francs or to 4,000 shillings. This makes a provision of Swiss francs 2,80 per week per head (or 2 shillings, seven pence per week); or 30 Swiss centimes per head per day (or some 4 ½ pence per day).

The rent and other expenses have to be met from this *sum* as is stated in the ultimate paragraph of Thomson's report.

Would it astound anyone if those destitute were to perish within a few months?

Victims of massacre in Mosul and villages.

85. In addition to the above destitute, there are many other thousands in

(1) The streets of Mosul and
(2) In the ruined villages.

Both those classes of destitute are uncared for. Those in Mosul are left to die from famine, nakedness and disease. Those in the villages, who for the same reasons are being exterminated, are not less than 6,500. The Iraq Government in a statement to the League of Nations says that those in the villages have been helped. The amount of this help is tabulated below for the easy reference of the reader.

Mumber of villages said ot have received assistance 36	Total number of population 5,431	Total monetary assistance (Dinars) 628 or Swiss frs. 1.85 per person

Seeds.

Wheat in kilos 39,368 or 7.248 per person	Barley in kilos 14,630 or 2.693 per person	Total number of mules 4 or 1.357 persons to a mule

Total number of oxen 62 or 87 persons to an ox.	Total number of blankets issued 357 or 15 persons to a Blanket

Cereals for Food.

Cereals for Food Wheat	Barley	Total number of agricultural implements
Total number of kilos 28,728 or 5.289 to a person	Total number of kilos 34,580 or 6.367 to a person	62 or 87 persons to one implement

It is on this quantity of grain that the Assyrians are required to survive for several months until they are transported from Iraq to some other country. The provision allowed for each person is hardly sufficient for one week.

Assyrian belongings before the massacre.

86. Before the massacre, every Assyrian family normally possessed, in addition to cash:

20 to	100 sheep.
2 to	6 oxen.
1 to	5 cows.
1 to	3 mules.
1 to	2 horses.

2,260 to 13,560 kilos of grain.
Cooking utensils, bedding, house furniture, etc.

Material losses during and after the massacre.

87. The following table shows material losses of the Assyrians during and after the massacre. 2,000 families were affected by the massacre and the scale given below is an average of losses *per family*.

	Rupees
50 sheep at 6 rupees[1] per sheep	600,000
1 mule at 120 rupees a mule	240,000
Total horses 600 at 144 rupees a horse	86,400
1 ox at 24 rupees an ox	48,000
Total cows 600 at 36 rupees each	21,600
Total donkeys 200 at rupees 12 each	2,400
House furniture at rupees 120 each	240,000
Wheat 20 toghars at 5 rupees a toghar	200,000
Barley 20 Toghars at rupees 1/4 a toghar	50,000
Cash Rs 120 per family	240,000
Ornaments and articles of value per family rupees 24 each	48,000
Total	1,776,400[2]

1. 13 rupees to a pound.
2. or 136,646 pounds for the total of the 2,000 families, or £68/6/5 ½ per family.

The End.

In his numerous reports from Baghdad, Cyprus and Geneva, the Mar Shimun, Patriarch of the Assyrians, placed before the League of Nations the case of his people and the Council of the League dealt with them on October 14th, 1933, during its 77th session.

Yasin's connection with the massacre.

88. The Iraqi representative, Yasin al Hashimi, stated that "The Iraqi Government did not wish to conceal that excesses had been committed; it deplored them no less sincerely than the governments represented on the Council".

Few people perhaps know that Yasin who 'sincerely deplored the excesses' was one of the paramount instigators of the massacre. Moreover, the Iraqi Prime Minister, Rashid 'Ali al Gailani, drove in a car in the streets of Mosul with Bakr Sidqy, the Arab assassin commander.

Mar Shimun asks for independent commission of enquiry.

89. The Mar Shimun made it quite clear that without an independent enquiry commission on the spot, the situation of those Assyrians still remaining in Iraq would go from bad to worse.

The Six Power Committee.

90. On October 13th, M. de Madariaga in his capacity as Rapporteur to the Council submitted a report to the Council which was adopted. This included the following recommendations pending the emigration of the Assyrians from Iraq.

"Having regard to the profound anxiety that has been caused by recent events, I trust that, until it has been possible to put into effect the arrangements outlined above, the Iraqi Government will be good enough to keep the Committee regularly informed of the measures taken to ensure:

(*a*) The safety of the Assyrians in Iraq;
(*b*) To assist the families left destitute in consequence of those events and

(*c*) To rebuild those villages which have been wholly or partly destroyed through the same events.

A committee composed of six members (Denmark, France, Italy, Mexico, Spain and Great Britain), was appointed by the Council in order to prepare and take the necessary measures for the execution of a plan for the establishment of the Assyrians outside Iraq. This committee held its first meeting on October 17th.

Possible places of emigration

91. In the meantime, oppression of the Assyrians continues, and individual murders, after the natural cessation of the massacre, have become more frequent in the space of a few weeks than during any previous year. The League of Nations was regularly furnished by the Mar Shimun with reports in regard to such occurrences, and as no protection could be afforded—even during this interval—the Mar Shimun on the 25th of October submitted proposals of possible places which would, under the circumstances be suitable to the Assyrians, in the absence of better arrangements. These places, in order of preference, were:

1. Syria.
2. Brazil.
3. Argentine.
4. Cyprus.
5. Palestine.
6. Canada.

Nos. 4 and 5 were considered by the Mar Shimun undesirable for economic and political reasons respectively.

Kurdish-Assyrian enclave.

92. Before making the above suggestions, the Mar Shimun in his report dated 8th of October, 1933, to the League of Nations stated:
"If it should be possible at this late date, to form (as suggested by Lord Curzon Dec. 17, 1919) a "Kurdish-Assyrian enclave in the north of the

Wilayet of Mosul under special administration, where Kurds and Assyrians might dwell together we would accept that solution."

Proposals to safeguard Assyrian interests during the interval.

93. On the other hand, on the 24th of October the Mar Shimun submitted to the League of Nations his suggestions and proposals as to how emigration could be made a success, for there is every reason to believe that steps will be taken (and as a matter of fact such steps are already being taken) to prevent as many Assyrians as possible from leaving Iraq for both financial and political reasons.

The Mar Shimun's suggestions were as follows:

(1) A general amnesty proclamation to be issued by the Iraq Government to cover all alleged offences in regard to:

   (*a*) Assyrian National movement and /or
   (*b*) All alleged offences resulting from the settlement scheme.

(2) Assyrian leaders now under Government detention to be set free and allowed to return to their homes pending emigration.

(3) Effective measures to be taken by the League of Nations to stop the present individual murders.

(4) Urgent steps to be taken to send a relief committee to Iraq to remove misery from thousands of Assyrians who are left homeless and destitute.

(5) An Enquiry Commission appointed by the League of Nations to proceed to Iraq with full powers to enquire into the reasons leading up to the recent massacre of the Assyrians; the extent of the excesses committed, and define the responsibility of the two parties concerned.

(6) The Assyrians to be assured, by the Enquiry Commission, full liberty to speak, and their safety to be adequately safeguarded until they leave Iraq territory.

(7) A special emigration committee to be set up under the auspices of the League of Nations to remain in Iraq until migration is successfully completed.

(8) The Assyrian Patriarch to be allowed to return to Iraq to help the Emigration Committee. Provision for his safety to be made.

(9) Assyrians possessing Mulk lands (privately owned lands) or any other privately owned immoveable property, wishing to leave Iraq, to have their mulk valued by the League's Commission or by a sub-committee and paid for by the Iraq Government.

    (*a*) This similarly applies to Assyrian Waqf property (property of charitable or religious institutions).

(10) Full indemnity to the relatives of persons massacred, other than those actually killed in action on the Iraq-Syro frontier.

    (*a*) Valuation of and payment for all Assyrian property moveable or immoveable, looted or destroyed.

(11) Iraqis indebted to Assyrians should settle such outstanding debts prior to emigration and/or such debts should be collected by the new State accepting the Assyrians on their behalf in accordance with a procedure to be laid down for the purpose in agreement with the Government of Iraq.

(12) Assyrians forced to embrace Islam or Assyrian women kept by Iraqi troops or Muslim population to be set free.

(13) A new country, other than Iraq, to be found under the auspices of the League of Nations for the new settlement of the Assyrians in a manner that should avoid the repetition of the very near past i.e. permanent peace and security for the Assyrians and not to be used for any political ends.

(13)A. Agricultural and medical aspects to be among other main considerations.

(14) Open door to Assyrian refugees, from all countries, wishing to establish themselves in the new Assyrian settlement on conditions to be agreed upon with the Government concerned."

It has been authoritatively learned that the League of nations approached various Governments (including that of Canada which for climatic reasons and owing to its proximity to other Assyrian colonies would have been very suitable) but no Government other than that of Brazil offered to open its doors until now. For this humanitarian act, every Assyrians owes deep gratitude to the Brazilian Government.

An appeal to America.

94. Various suggestions from different sources have been made, but the fact that "The Assyrians, under the present circumstances, are not given the choice and can only take what they are given" seems to be the essential element lacking in those suggestions. There is no doubt that if the United States of America, whose humanitarian work has exceeded any other, would be good enough to accept the Assyrian refugees, this would be the most agreable solution. There are already in the U.S.A. some 20,000 Assyrians who have flourished and are happy citizens of that country. If the American Government were to consider such a proposal with a sympathetic eye, it would save a Nation in its entirety.

Among the suggestions made is that concerning Erivan. This suggestion is worth while consideration in view of the fact that there are already in Russia some 40,000 Assyrians and because the only desire of the Assyrians is to live in peace.

Hakkiari, the original home of the Assyrians, has also been suggested. The desire of the Assyrians to return thither would no doubt be unanimous. Hakkiari can only be bought but such a possibility seems out of question.

Resolution of the Six Power Committee.

95. On November 16th, 1933, the Committee of Six adopted a resolution that "It is the intention of the Government of Iraq to appoint a local commission, consisting of the expert in rural settlement, Major Thomson, of a local officer of the Government of Iraq and of the head of the Assyrian village concerned. This commission will explain to the Assyrians the precise significance of the decision of the Council of the League which contemplated the establishment outside Iraq of the Assyrians who expressed a desire to abandon the country. The Commission will further inform the populations concerned that a committee of the Council is actively considering plans with a view to giving effect to the Council decision.

"As soon as possible after the place of settlement has definitely been fixed, a representative of the Nansen office for Refugees, appointed by the office in agreement with the Chairman of the Council committee, will proceed to Iraq in order to co-operate with the local commission and the various authorities.

"The instructions issued under this arrangement are as follows:

(*a*) To ascertain who are the persons desiring to leave the country;
(*b*) To take all the necessary measures for their departure, such as liquidation of their property, the participation of those who wish to emigrate in the cost of transport and settlement, the transport of the emigrants from their homes, etc.

"It is understood that detailed reports on the work done will be addressed to the Council Committee through the Government of Iraq."

On November 30th, 1933, under letter No. 19/4, sent from London, the Patriarch drew the attention of the President of the Committee of Six to the inefficaciousness of the above resolution in the following sense:

"I presume that the Commission presided over by Major Thomson is only empowered to do preliminary work until the arrival of the Nansen's representative. If this is not so, and if the emigration of the Assyrians should lie in the hands of a commission under Major Thomson, assisted by two other members also in the pay of the Iraq Government, it is quite obvious that this majority of three cannot be expected to safeguard the interests of the Assyrians. In view of the recent past and the consequences of the dealings of the Assyrians with Major Thomson and the Iraq Government this year, you will, I hope, realize that my people cannot have confidence in the impartiality of such a commission. It is entirely impossible for the Assyrians to lay their interests in the hands of an organ controlled by the Iraq Government.

"In undertaking such a great scheme as the emigration of thousands of people, no one can hope for a successful conclusion, if the emigrants cannot have complete confidence in the machinery set up to decide the details of the emigration. I sincerely hope that the Council of the League of Nations will not set up this machinery definitely without enquiring whether or not the Assyrians have confidence in it."

As the Iraq Government has undertaken to bear a portion of the emigration expenses, it is taking illegal steps by various methods—only known to those who know the country and its people—to make the emigration impossible in order to reduce its financial share and to justify its gross misrepresentations made from time to time.

The Assyrian levy problem.

96. On the other hand, the question of the Assyrian levies is no doubt one of the most important outstanding elements which will hinder the smooth working of the emigration scheme. The reasons have been very ably summarised by Dr. Wigram[1] in the following words:

"The Air-Marshal demanded 'either British troops or Assyrian levies' for the ground guard of his establishments in Iraq."

This statement of the Air-Marshal was made during the Assyrian levy resignation in 1932. The reasons which led him to make this remark still maintain and it is hoped that this policy will not be insisted upon if the wish to save the remaining remnant is sincere.

The families and relatives of the Assyrian levies solely depend after the massacre on the levies for maintenance. There are 750 levies at present with some 8,000 immediate dependents. The monthly pay of a levy is 25[1] rupees a month. With this pay he must support his family and relatives. To quote an instance.

Levy soldier X has a wife and 4 children. His two brothers Y and Z fell victims to the massacre, leaving some 10 persons dependent on X. Everything Y and Z possessed was either looted or destroyed. X will be asked to renew his service contract for a year or for some indefinite period. If he signs, he and his relatives will automatically be retained in Iraq. If he refuses to sign, he and his relatives must face death through starvation.

Suffice to say that the home in which the Assyrians lived for thousands of years where they preserved their existence for centuries under Persians, Sassanites and where the Turk protected them, the people with whom they fought side by side for the common cause during the war and trusted and served them subsequently cannot protect them. They therefore have to be transplanted in Brazil or elsewhere.

———————